FAMILIA

FA

MARCELA VALLADOLID

MILIA

125 FOOLPROOF MEXICAN RECIPES TO FEED YOUR PEOPLE

PHOTOGRAPHS BY
ISABELLA MARTINEZ-FUNCKE

VORACIOUS

Little, Brown and Company
New York Boston London

*This book is dedicated to the
thousands of students who inspired me
to develop and teach these recipes—
also known as mi familia.*

CONTENTS

APPETIZERS /
Botanas 25

SALADS /
Ensaladas 39

TRADITIONAL FLAVORS /
Sabores Tradicionales 55

DINNERS
en Casa Marcela 105

TACOS DE SALMÓN (PAGE 129)

FOREWORD

arcela, my younger sister, my best friend, my life partner and greatest source of inspiration as a woman, gave me the honor of writing this foreword.

A few months after the pandemic arrived in March 2020, Marcela and I felt totally disconnected. Then by luck I arrived one day at Marcela's house and she spontaneously pulled me into a live show she was doing on Instagram, where she was making an oven-roasted chicken. At the end of the show, we received hundreds of messages asking if we could please do something together again for the public.

It is worth mentioning that I do not cook. AT ALL. But the balance of our gifts yielded a very promising recipe. We created the "Marcela & Carina Show," a Zoom-based cookalong, with a finely chosen intention as our sole purpose: *connection*.

We had no idea how we would do that through a computer screen, but after more than one hundred recipes from Marcela and thirty episodes, all sold out, we found ourselves part of an interwoven community of thousands who were moved to cook alongside us. I am so grateful for this portal for connection, community, and getting in touch with our roots that it moves me to tears.

In this book, you will enter the magical world of Marcela's kitchen, full of love and creativity and joy. Her teaching skill and her great love for cooking, her people, and Mexican culture create a space where we can simply live in the now.

I am amazed to see how Marcela can teach anyone, even those who believe that they don't know how to cook (like yours truly), to become a fabulous cook without even realizing it. These recipes are the result of all those classes in which Marcela led her students to trust their intuition, to trust themselves. "If you make a mistake, do it again." "If you think it lacks salt, just add more!"

As we said so often in class: "NO PASA NADA!" — "NOTHING HAPPENS!"

Marcela wants more than anything in this world for her students to surpass her. This collection of recipes is evidence. Tested and cooked by thousands of home cooks, they can be trusted to lead you to success.

The reader of this book will feel the intention with which each of these recipes was given life, and the love with which they were created. There is an amazing story in each one of them. Through these flavors, textures, and smells, you, the student, already a cook, will receive them as medicine for the soul.

Thank you, Marcela, because every time I enter your kitchen, you give me the gift of finding myself.

—CARINA LUZ VALLADOLID

INTRODUCTION

La Cocina Matriarca

My mother was a true matriarca. My father provided for the family, but she was *there*. She ran our lives. She decided what we did every day. Where we went to school. What parties we could go to. How late we could stay at those parties. Who was allowed to come over. And she absolutely decided what we ate. She was the CEO of our home.

She passed shortly after I sold my first book to a publisher, at the beginning of my culinary journey. You would think that I took her example with me and applied it, but at so many steps of the way, I didn't.

As a Mexican cook trying to make it in America, I felt I simply didn't have the voice to fight back when something felt inauthentic. I used to think I had to change who I was to find an audience. Not by a lot, just an inch here, an inch there. It led to sometimes choosing a "mainstream" approach instead of something truer to me…just so a mass audience might find it more appealing.

My work life became more about fitting in than making trouble. Instead of standing up, I often shrank down. I delivered on deadlines. I showed up on time and knew my lines. But I pushed down my creativity and authenticity while I did what I thought I had to do to stay in the game.

This book and these recipes are what happened when I let go of all those expectations and just *cooked*. That is, when I stopped trying to do something to a standard that someone else set, and simply cooked for myself, and for my people—the ones who matter the most.

When the pandemic hit, like most of planet earth, I had to sit back and evaluate what I was doing and why. What started as a way to distract myself from what felt like the end of humanity (let's be real, that's what it felt like) morphed into a project that would put me and my very best friend on earth, my sister Carina, in front of our beloved community cooking *only* the food that I fed my people.

Twice a month, we opened up my kitchen to about a thousand students online to distract ourselves from the challenges outside our doors. We quickly realized it wasn't just about the food, it was about creating space for our community to cook and celebrate our culture with zero assumptions or expectations. The only goal was to have *fun*.

The feedback was unanimous: our students told us that they were cooking food that transported them to their childhood.

Everything I've done before this has filled me with pride—the books, the TV shows, all of it. And even though it's certainly not perfect, I wouldn't change that journey. I like it here. I like it now. But the absolute magic and gift of sharing the food that I found most appealing in those classes is that it connected with *you* more than anything I had ever done before.

Even better, the recipes became a tool for empowerment. They helped me reclaim my power in the kitchen, and step into my own role as matriarca. They did the same for you, and I'm so grateful that you've shared those stories with me.

What in many ways has been seen as a chore that kept women at home and in the kitchen became a source of pride and connection to our culture. As we made these recipes, we stripped them of all the baggage and cooked to bring *joy* and *connection*.

In this book, you'll find some dishes that I never had the courage to propose to cook on TV. From Bacalao a la Vizcaina to Tesmole or tortillas from scratch (too complicated for a TV audience), these recipes reflect how so many of us preserve our roots and memories by cooking.

I am uncomfortable with the word "ambassador" or with the responsibility of preserving history or tradition. I am simply a Mexicana living in San Diego who is so ridiculously proud of her Tijuana upbringing that I continue to cook the foods that take me back home.

Everyone is invited to this fiesta. I don't care who you are or where you come from; you *can* cook these foods and love them and make them a part of your life. I'm done with this idea that only certain people can cook certain foods. All you need is a willingness to respect and understand our culture. Go out and get yourself a molcajete and make some fresh salsa and post it on the 'gram as your own.

You'll hear my voice in the recipes, giving you a heads up about a tedious procedure or calming you down if a sauce breaks. I can get a little intense about certain things (I do love my flaky salt), but that's only because I want to ensure the best result.

I suggest that you follow recipes word for word in the beginning. But the ultimate goal is to build your self-confidence so that you can walk into the kitchen as a true matriarca, with nothing but your inner compass guiding your every move. In the words of William Arthur Ward, "The mediocre teacher tells. The good teacher explains. The superior teacher demonstrates. The great teacher inspires." I will continue in my personal pursuit of that greatness because if I can inspire *you*, you will then find your own ways to inspire others.

Now, go get that molcajete because every woman's (and man's) place *is* in the kitchen.

Gracias, familia! A cocinar!

But don't take my word for it…here are a few words to give you confidence from students who have cooked these dishes.

· · · · · · · · · ·

@Ginas3pollitos

Learning new secrets to all of these traditional recipes is irreplaceable BUT watching your family devour them with a smile—Priceless!

· · · · · · · · · ·

@laflower32

Cooking with Chef and Carina has instilled new excitement, curiosity, and pride in our cuisine…. My palate craves our food now more than ever and that's literally life altering, from one border girl to another.

· · · · · · · · · ·

@alisonbenji

Things I have learned from class: Mise en place is the key to success. Season in layers. Chiles do not have to burn your mouth to be tasty. Dance while you are cooking and share love through your food. Don't stress over the outcome; enjoy the process and it will work out.

· · · · · · · · · ·

@gmarlene

You and your cooking help me embrace our culture and traditions. Your recipe to Tacos al Pastor (my husband's favorite) has given me hope that I can cook authentic Mexican food just as delicious.

· · · · · · · · · ·

@knmcoon

Your recipes and techniques are beyond just cooking. They capture the true essence of our ancestors…I'm more excited and have the confidence to take my recipes to the next level. So much pride for our Mom's Grandmothers and Aunts who paved the way for us all.

· · · · · · · · · ·

@cortimenez70

I learned not to be afraid of attempting to cook like my mom. Unfortunately I wasn't able to learn all the Mexican cooking my mom did before she passed away. I was afraid it would be too hard to make my favorite Mexican dishes. Taking your classes taught me to take the chances and my favorites came out wonderful.

· · · · · · · · · ·

@alfiedoll

Season all, have confidence, it cannot go wrong… but if it does: no pasa nada!!!

· · · · · · · · · ·

@coralito18

Your classes taught me I don't have to be a chef to cook like one AND I've impressed my mom, who had the best sazón in the world.

· · · · · · · · · ·

@mexiguat1

I learned to have fun and not be intimidated about cooking something that seems complex because if you break it down into smaller steps… it's all very doable.

· · · · · · · · · ·

@naninat64

The thing I loved most about the recipes is that fact that you are so detailed it becomes foolproof…

· · · · · · · · · ·

@natureandtime

QUE NO PASA NADAAAA

SOPA DE ALBÓNDIGAS (PAGE 172)

GET
READY
TO COOK

As you may know, these recipes were developed to be taught live, as part of a complete menu, to thousands of folks in their own homes. I absolutely loved the challenge of cooking an entire menu within a 120-minute window. A delicate dance that I would choreograph a few minutes before going live with all the students. I have many faults as a chef; speed and organization are not two of them. I had a chef in culinary school who yelled about "THE PRINCIPLES OF TIME AND MOTION" as much as he yelled about a perfect chiffonade or the proper percentage of mirepoix.

In the cooking classes, I was often told to slow down, and I apologize for that. Actually, I don't, because in the end, faced with no other option, you all executed to perfection. You did make food in record time that was not only beautifully presented, but was also delicious. I saw it posted, tagged, and talked about on social media. Here, I'll share with you some of the tips I've shared with students or anyone I've ever mentored.

1. ***Read the recipe.*** READ THE RECIPE! I'm guilty of glossing over them at this point in my life, but knowing how a recipe is going to unfold without reading the whole thing only comes with experience. It seems so simple, but sometimes just reading it once or even twice and visualizing the steps will put you more at ease, especially if you're a novice.

2. ***MISE EN PLACE!*** Which translates roughly to "everything in its place." Again, once you feel more comfortable in the kitchen, you can prep in steps, such as save the chopping of veggies for the soup until after you've gotten your pot filled and it's on its way to boiling. Once you get the hang of a recipe, you'll identify pockets of time where you can prep as you go. But in the beginning, you will be much more successful if *all* your ingredients are chopped and measured before you even head to the stove.

3. ***Organize your ingredients.*** If you are cooking multiple recipes at a time, which is what most of us do DAILY when making dinner (or on the big cooking days like Thanksgiving or Las Posadas), I highly suggest you place the ingredients for each recipe on a separate baking sheet. I've always asked my students to do this, and they always come back saying the same thing: it's a GAME CHANGER!

4. ***Follow the recipe before you do your own thing.*** As much as my goal is to get you to a place where you don't need a recipe to cook, it takes time to work your way there. I'm not the most accessible when asked for substitutions when teaching because it CHANGES the recipe along with my intentions for flavor and presentation. So, do it the intended way first, so you can see and taste the goal. Then, get creative. Of course, if you have allergies or restrictions, do what you must! (I do get a little irked when asked to substitute the ingredient that *makes* the dish, like when I was asked to replace the chicken in a roast chicken recipe…You're just making a different dish at that point, which is cool, but I can't guarantee success when you make changes.)

5. ***Last but not least, come into the kitchen with good energy and good intentions.*** Carina would say this is the most important! Those of us who cook for a living or do it daily for our families *know* that food tastes better when prepared with love. It's like the energy is consumed in the same way as the actual ingredients. I steer clear of the kitchen when I'm not in a good head space, which means I miss deadlines, but if I don't feel good, I don't cook good.

Notes on Equipment

MOLCAJETE. A mortar and pestle made from lava rock. It's worth repeating what I tell you in a recipe: as opposed to cutting through ingredients with a blade (as you would with a blender or processor), you're literally grinding flavors, oils, and aromas OUT of ingredients. The friction between the molcajete (the base) and the tejolote (the cylinder-like rock you hold in the palm of your hand) releases, for example, oils from nuts and seeds, which give your mole a deeper and more nuanced taste. It's just different. I mean, it's subtle but noticeable. There are a couple of recipes where I ask for just a processor, but any time grinding or blending takes place, you can reach for the molcajete.

HIGH-POWERED BLENDER. One of the phrases I repeat to my students is "A good chef is determined by the texture of her sauces," and I mean it! Even if tradition allows or even calls for a grainy sauce, like in our most traditional Chiles en Nogada (page 66), I still give the direction to take the sauce to smooth and silky. I accomplish this with the help of my Vitamix. I've just found that machine to be the most reliable. I've owned only two in the last

twenty years, so for me, they work. Mole, by the way, can blow the motor on a weak blender. The only time I've ever had to change clothes while cooking live has been while blending a mole in a crappy blender that got jammed with a cinnamon stick. The bottom popped up and sprayed mole on my ivory-colored top. Good times. Invest in a blender. I don't advocate for much special equipment in the kitchen, but a powerful blender is a *must*.

HEAVY BAKING SHEETS. Another item worth an investment. I prefer heavy, rimmed commercial-grade half sheet pans that don't rust or warp at high temperatures. I use them for everything from cookies to roasting turkeys. If well treated, they last for years, and the even heat distribution of a heavy baking sheet will give you consistent results. I have always liked either Williams Sonoma or Nordic Ware's natural aluminum commercial rimmed baking sheets.

TORTILLA PRESS. This is important. If you want to ensure you are getting a well-calibrated tortilla press, then you're going to pay a little more. Can you get lucky and score a good one for a few bucks at the Mercado Hidalgo in Tijuana? Absolutely. But my suggestion is to make the investment on a piece that will last a lifetime. You are correct in thinking that cocineras across Mexico are not buying expensive tortilla presses, but let's not compare ourselves to women with levels of expertise that come from handling masa since shortly after birth. Most of them, in fact, don't even use a press. They can get to a perfectly even ¹/₈-inch-thick tortilla by using the palms of their hands, gently tossing and slapping the masa from one side to the other. They make it look so easy, but go ahead and try it! Evenness is important because you want the tortilla to puff after a turn on the comal. The puff means you've managed to trap steam inside the tortilla, which will ensure its proper cooking. Tortilla-making is an art and a good press is a great tool for the beginner to master it.

Notes on Ingredients

SALT. Specifically flaky sea salt. It's the only thing I use for cooking. I specifically love Maldon sea salt and have been telling my students to use it since I discovered it years ago. The goal is to find an "unsalty" salt, if that makes sense. That's what I love about this brand: you don't *taste* the salt. It does a good job of making the ingredients the stars. It's like an overzealous stage mom, just encouraging you from the darkness at the side of the stage, never seen by anyone really but getting you to perform at your very best. Salt is, by far, the most important ingredient in your kitchen. Find yourself a good one! Note that if you are using kosher salt or table salt instead, reduce the volume of salt a recipe calls for by as much as half. Because those salts have smaller grains, you get much more saltiness in a teaspoon.

NOPALES. Cactus paddles. They grow all over California; I have a small one in the entry of my house, but I buy them at the market. Cleaning them of their spikes is a pain, and a beginner can seriously get hurt. I prefer to purchase them cleaned and chopped into cubes. Look for bright green, firm, crisp pieces that are not soft and slimy. It's an acquired taste, but one you'd be smart to get into! They are packed with fiber and very filling, and if you have any left over, you can throw them into a smoothie. They have a clean and grassy taste and are very good when cleaned of their slime and cooked properly.

JAMAICA. Hibiscus. I grew up drinking agua de jamaica all day, every day. It's the reason I find it so hard to drink water: jamaica was my hydration. It's tart and bitter and you can sweeten it as much or as little as you like. I go for an actual cup of sugar (or more) per pitcher, but you can use agave or stevia or monk fruit or any other sweetener and in smaller amounts. I buy the flowers in bulk and store them in a giant glass jar because of their beautiful burgundy color. When used to make an agua fresca, the concentrate is meant to be heavy and not at all like the tea at Starbucks! The flowers are usually discarded after they are used to make the agua, but I use them to make salsa and as the filling for tacos.

PILONCILLO. Unprocessed cane sugar usually shaped like a cone. To replace one piloncillo cone, take $1/2$ cup of packed dark brown sugar and add 1 tablespoon of dark molasses. Depending on the moisture level of piloncillo, it can be very easy or very difficult to chop or grate. Don't worry if you can only get a coarse chop out of it. It will all melt in the heat anyway.

MASA. This topic could take up an entire book, but I'll keep it simple. When purchasing masa, *read the label*. Masa for tamales has fat (lard); masa for tortillas does not. They are both made with corn but are NOT interchangeable. If your masa seems a little dry when you get it home, you can certainly add a little more water to the tortilla masa, or more fat or water/broth to the tamal masa. Most Mexican markets make and sell very good-quality fresh masa. I suggest purchasing it the same day you will cook with it.

CHILES. Instead of explaining the characteristics of each chile (Google is your friend), I want to explain why I add either "fresh" or "dried" to a chile's description in the ingredients list. You might find it odd that I call for a "dried" guajillo as there is no such thing as a "fresh" guajillo. But for the novice cook in the Mexican kitchen, the chiles can be the most confusing part! A chile's name will change from fresh to dried to smoked, and by adding either "fresh" or "dried," I'm directing you to a specific section at the market. In terms of heat level, I'm relaxed about switching things up to make a dish friendly to your and your family's palate. Swap a serrano for a jalapeño if you want it hotter and add only half of the chiles de árbol to the salsa if you don't want to feel like your tongue is about to ignite. We like that feeling. It feels like home.

MEXICAN OREGANO. Is it actually different than Greek/Mediterranean oregano? The difference is subtle, but Mexican oregano has more of a citrusy profile than true oregano, which is more minty. Taste them side by side to notice the difference, and you'll see!

"YOUR FAVORITE SEASONING." I say this. A lot. Mine happens to be a commercial brand that mixes onion powder, garlic powder, sugar, and a little natural hickory smoke, but you can easily just stick to salt and pepper with a pinch of any or all of these. I didn't grow up eating spices, nothing dried was ever added other than oregano or bay leaves but, and this is a BIG BUT, we added MSG-laden chicken bouillon to EVERYTHING. I have never added bouillon to a published recipe. I go with the aforementioned mix of spices and sometimes add either nutritional yeast or mushroom-based seasonings for that umami flavor. There are mixed ideas about MSG being bad for you or not. I steer clear of it.

ACHIOTE. There are a couple of recipes where I ask for this ground-up annatto seed seasoning that comes in a little brick. It's readily available online and my only note on its usage is to make sure you give it enough time to cook so that you can't taste it. Raw achiote is a totally different experience than when it's cooked, low and slow, with citrus and other seasonings. It should be subtle and almost not identifiable to your palate.

TO EAT OR NOT TO EAT? When it comes to underripe ingredients, there are some where I would, quite frankly, skip the recipe altogether rather than use an underripe ingredient. The two biggest ones are avocado and mango. An avocado should offer little resistance when cutting and you should be able to easily pull off the peel with your hand. And mangoes with pale-yellow flesh are the devil.

APPETIZERS

Botanas

Guess what, these empanadas are baked and not fried, but they are nevertheless packed with so much flavor. It's very easy to make the empanada dough; just adhere to the rest times and really work the dough to get to a soft texture before you roll it out. You might want to give up, but don't stop till it's no longer grainy!

These are filled with picadillo, but rajas or chicken in salsa verde or a slice of cheese with cooked chorizo or sautéed mushrooms and Brie—or anything your heart desires—can be used as a filling. Whatever you choose, you will need about 2 tablespoons per empanada, or about 1½ cups for ten to twelve of them.

DOUGH

2⅓ cups all-purpose flour, plus more for dusting

1 tablespoon granulated sugar

1 teaspoon flaky sea salt

½ teaspoon baking powder

10 tablespoons unsalted butter, cubed, chilled

½ cup crema Mexicana

1 large egg

FOR ASSEMBLY

1 recipe Picadillo (recipe follows), cooled

1 large egg, whisked, to brush over the empanadas

Fresh salsa or salsa macha, to serve

Preheat the oven to 350°F and line a large rimmed baking sheet with a silicone mat or parchment paper.

To make the dough, in a food processor, pulse the flour, sugar, salt, and baking powder until combined. Add the butter and process until you have a coarse meal and the mixture begins to stick to the side of the container, about 2 minutes. Transfer to a large bowl and stir in the crema and egg, using a wooden spoon. When combined, turn out onto a floured surface and knead until smooth, about 3 minutes. Divide the dough into two equal parts, cover tightly with plastic wrap, and refrigerate for 10 minutes.

Take half of the dough and roll out to ¼-inch thickness on a floured surface. Using a 5- to 5½-inch bowl as a guide, cut disks from the dough and transfer to the prepared baking sheet. You can reroll the dough trimmings to get one or two more entire disks.

To assemble, fill each dough disk with 2 tablespoons of picadillo. Brush the edges lightly with egg and fold into half-moons. Pinch the edges to seal the empanadas. Brush the empanadas with more egg. Refrigerate the empanadas 5 to 15 minutes.

Bake until golden, about 35 minutes. Serve hot with any fresh salsa or salsa macha.

EMPANADAS *de* PICADILLO

PICADILLO

There's so much controversy around the origins of this very simple dish. You'll find versions across Latin America, some with raisins or olives or pimientos or all the above. Some are sweeter, like the picadillo we make in Mexico to stuff poblanos for chiles en nogada. Some are very soupy, some are dry. I'm sharing with you the version I grew up with in Tijuana. A big Tupperware container of this would always be in our fridge, and we scooped it into corn tortillas for soft tacos with pickled jalapeños and avocado, for tostadas, just over rice or on its own. Cold. Straight out of the container. At four a.m. after a night of dancing at Baby Rock (Tijuana's #1 nightclub in the '90s). TMI. Anyway, picadillo is so easy. And so good. *Makes 5 to 6 cups, 4 to 6 servings (more than plenty for 10 to 12 empanadas)*

2 tablespoons extra-virgin olive oil, divided

1 large vine-ripened tomato, cut into chunks

1 large dried ancho chile, stemmed, seeded, and ripped into small pieces

½ cup low-sodium chicken broth

½ large white onion, minced (about ¾ cup)

½ large russet potato, peeled, cut into ½- to ¼-inch pieces

2 garlic cloves, minced

1½ pounds lean ground beef

½ cup chopped fresh parsley

Salt and freshly ground black pepper

Heat 1 tablespoon of the oil in a large, heavy sauté pan over medium-high heat. Add the tomato and dried ancho, and cook for 5 minutes to release the juices. Add the broth, lower the heat, and simmer for 8 minutes. Transfer to a blender and blend until smooth. Set the puree aside.

Heat the remaining tablespoon of olive oil in a large, heavy sauté pan over medium-high heat. Add the onion, potato, and garlic and sauté for 4 minutes. Add the meat and sauté for 4 minutes, making sure to really break the meat apart, using a wooden spoon. Add the tomato puree, lower the heat to medium-low, cover, and simmer for 10 minutes. Stir in the parsley and season to taste with salt and black pepper.

This is seared meat served chilled with a citrusy soy-based sauce with serranos and avocados. It's easy to make, different and delicious. Tijuana, where I grew up, has a significant Asian influence in its cuisine because one of the largest communities of Chinese immigrants in Mexico is in Mexicali nearby.

Aguachile refers to a spicy citrus-cured raw protein. It's similar to ceviche but goes heavier on the chile, and usually has the addition of some liquid, such as water or salsa. It's traditionally made with shrimp, but what I'm doing here with steak is a trend now in Mexico; you can find it in restaurants across the country. If I feel that it needs a little something earthy and fatty, I will top it with thinly sliced green onions that I dust in flour and fry. That is totally optional! ***Serves 4 as an appetizer***

½ red onion, thinly sliced (about 1 cup)

¼ cup extra-virgin olive oil, divided

2 tablespoons red wine vinegar

2¾ teaspoons flaky sea salt, divided, plus more for serving

1 teaspoon freshly ground black pepper, divided

1 1-pound boneless ribeye steak (1⅓ inches thick)

½ cup freshly squeezed lime juice

3 tablespoons freshly squeezed orange juice

2 teaspoons soy sauce

1⅛-ounce fresh serrano chile, seeds and ribs removed, finely chopped (about 1¼ teaspoons), plus thin slices for serving

1 garlic clove, finely chopped

1 medium avocado, pitted, peeled, and diced (about ¾ cup)

Tostadas, for serving

Toss together the red onion, 2 tablespoons of the olive oil, the vinegar, ½ teaspoon of the salt, and ¼ teaspoon of the black pepper in a medium bowl. Cover and chill until ready to serve.

Heat a 12-inch cast-iron skillet over medium-high heat. Season the steak all over with 1½ teaspoons of the salt and ½ teaspoon of the black pepper. Add 1 tablespoon of the olive oil to the skillet; swirl to coat. Add the steak and cook, undisturbed, until a brown crust forms, about 5 minutes per side. Transfer the steak to a cutting board and let rest for 10 minutes.

While the steak rests, stir together the lime juice, orange juice, soy sauce, chopped serrano, garlic, remaining ¾ teaspoon of salt, remaining ¼ teaspoon of black pepper, and remaining tablespoon of olive oil in a small bowl. Transfer ¼ cup of the mixture to a separate small bowl, to reserve for serving.

Slice the steak against the grain between ¼ and ½ inch thick, transfer to a baking dish, and pour the remaining ½ cup of the citrus mixture over the steak to marinate it. Cover and chill for 30 minutes to 1 hour.

Remove the onion from its pickling liquid. Remove the steak from the marinade, transfer to a serving platter, and drizzle with the reserved ¼ cup of the citrus mixture. Garnish with the pickled onion, avocado, and sliced serrano. Sprinkle with salt. Serve with tostadas.

RIBEYE AGUACHILE

So simple, so fresh. And yes: you can use just about any white fish here! Just make sure it is sushi-grade and fresh. I love the clean taste and tender flesh of halibut, but it's expensive. Sole, flounder, snapper, mahi-mahi, rockfish, sea bass, fluke, or even a fatty mackerel will work. I have moved away from using farm-raised tilapia because of the antibiotics involved in the process. Sustainable wild-caught fish is my preference.

The fish goes raw into the dish. The acid from the limes changes the structure of the proteins in the fish, "cooking" it without heat. But you can overcook fish with lime juice, too! If the fish sits in the acidic liquid too long, it will break down and fall apart. *Serves 2 to 4*

1½ pounds skinless, boneless halibut (or other white fish), cut into ½-inch cubes

½ cup freshly squeezed lime juice

1 tablespoon extra-virgin olive oil

Flaky sea salt

5 medium tomatillos, husked and rinsed

1 fresh jalapeño chile, stemmed and seeded (for less heat)

1 fresh serrano chile, stemmed and seeded (for less heat)

¼ cup packed fresh cilantro

Freshly ground black pepper

2 medium cucumbers, peeled, seeded, and chopped

2 medium avocados, pitted, peeled, and diced

½ medium white onion, chopped

¼ cup finely chopped fresh cilantro leaves, for serving

Tostadas, for serving

Mayonnaise, for serving

In a large bowl, combine the halibut cubes, lime juice, and olive oil. Sprinkle with 1 teaspoon salt. Mix until the fish is evenly coated. Cover and refrigerate for about 25 minutes.

In a blender, combine the tomatillos, jalapeño, serrano, and packed ¼ cup of cilantro. Blend until a salsa consistency. Season to taste with salt and black pepper. Add this salsa verde to the bowl of fish and toss. Add the cucumbers, avocados, and onion and mix. Season the ceviche to taste with additional salt and black pepper, and garnish with the chopped cilantro leaves.

Serve with tostadas spread with mayonnaise, and enjoy.

HALIBUT CEVICHE VERDE

TACOS de JAMAICA

Many of us know jamaica (hibiscus) as an agua fresca. You will also find hibiscus-based salsas throughout Mexico, but here I turn it into a taco filling. When you cook hibiscus this way, it takes on the feeling of a protein, and is very filling and flavorful. The flowers are definitely tart, but that's why I add piloncillo, which takes it from tart to perfectly balanced.

Make sure to get a package of dehydrated flowers, usually sold in the produce section, and not tea bags that contain ground or processed flowers. You must boil the hibiscus to rehydrate it. Every time you boil it in fresh water, it loses some of its tartness. I boil the hibiscus only once, but I *really* like its tart flavor. You could easily boil the hibiscus two or three times to make it less tart. After boiling, you will be left with the liquid concentrate, so use it as the base for Jamaica and Mint Agua Fresca (page 221).

Salsa macha is so important for this taco because the smoky, oily macha brings the tart hibiscus into balance.

Chapulines are salted, dried, fried grasshoppers that are operate like a seasoned salt: they add a salty, savory crunch. If serving this to your familia: crush the chapulines first so the diners can't tell what they are. After they devour the tacos, tell them they just ate insects. Have a camera phone ready to capture their reactions. Post it. Tag me! *Serves 4 to 6*

2½ cups dehydrated hibiscus flowers

5 cups water

1 8-ounce piloncillo cone (if you can chop it, great; if not it will dissolve when cooked)

¼ cup balsamic vinegar

1 tablespoon extra-virgin olive oil

1 medium white onion, chopped (about 1 cup)

3 garlic cloves, pressed

1 fresh serrano chile, sliced into thin rounds

Salt and freshly ground black pepper

¼ cup chopped fresh cilantro

FOR ASSEMBLY

2 medium avocados, pitted, peeled, and sliced

8 to 10 warm corn tortillas

Extra-virgin olive oil

Salt

Salsa macha (optional)

Chapulines (optional)

Lime wedges

Combine the dehydrated hibiscus and water in a medium saucepan and bring to a boil over high heat. Lower the heat to medium-low and simmer for 5 minutes. Let stand for 10 minutes. Drain, reserving the rehydrated hibiscus and its concentrate separately.

Place ½ cup of the hibiscus concentrate in a small saucepan along with the piloncillo cone and balsamic vinegar and bring to a boil over high heat. Boil until reduced to ½ cup, about 15 minutes.

Heat the olive oil in a large, heavy sauté pan over high heat. Add the onion and sauté for 4 minutes, or till translucent. Add the garlic and serrano and sauté for 2 minutes longer. Add the rehydrated hibiscus and sauté for 10 minutes, stirring occasionally. Add the hibiscus reduction and simmer, uncovered, over low heat until all the liquid is evaporated, 10 to 12 minutes. Season to taste with salt and black pepper. Stir in the cilantro.

To assemble the tacos, spread some avocado on half of a tortilla and drizzle with a little olive oil and salt. Scoop some of the hibiscus filling over the avocado. Top with salsa macha, crushed chapulines, and a squeeze of lime juice, and eat!

GAME CHANGER

@vivianscocina

Using jamaica for tacos! Life changing. Why did we always throw them out after making jamaica agua fresca? Now I use them for everything like salsas, marinades, tacos, tinga, etc.!

This traditional Mexican dish is found in every coastal city across the country, often served with saltines. The addition of orange soda comes from the folks in Yucatán. It adds a sweet, citrusy kick that you can't tell is soda—it disappears—but I like to kick it up a bit with blood orange soda instead.

A coctel de camarón is different from a traditional American steakhouse shrimp cocktail. You're looking for a much runnier, soupier consistency that is a much more harmonious way of eating shrimp. You don't get a harsh horseradish-ketchup situation. Instead of being overwhelmed by one flavor, you experience a perfect combination of the flavors that are used repeatedly on the coasts of Mexico, like Clamato, cucumber, and lime. *Serves 4*

½ medium white onion

2 bay leaves

1 large carrot, halved

1 celery rib, halved

10 black peppercorns

10 green peppercorns

1 pound shrimp, peeled, deveined, with tails on

COCKTAIL SAUCE

½ cup chopped fresh cilantro

¼ cup chopped onion

1 cup diced cucumber with no seeds

½ cup chopped tomato with no seeds

¼ cup Clamato juice

½ cup ketchup

¼ cup blood orange or orange soda

2 tablespoons chipotles in adobo (just the sauce; add chopped chipotles for more heat)

1 tablespoon distilled white vinegar

1 tablespoon extra-virgin olive oil

Juice of ½ lemon

1 fresh serrano chile, stemmed, seeded, and minced

1 tablespoon hot sauce (Valentina, Cholula, Tamazula, or homemade)

Flaky sea salt and freshly ground black pepper to taste

FOR SERVING

1 medium avocado, pitted, peeled, and diced

Saltines or tortilla chips

Hot sauce

Lime wedges

In a large pot, combine 8 cups of water, 1 tablespoon of salt, and the onion half, bay leaves, carrot, celery, and peppercorns. Bring to a boil over high heat. Add the shrimp and boil for 1 minute. Turn off the heat and let stand for 5 to 6 minutes, until just cooked through. Plunge the shrimp into a bowl of ice water to cool, then drain. Remove the tails, cut each shrimp into three pieces, and transfer to a large bowl.

To make the cocktail sauce, in a small bowl, stir together all the sauce ingredients. Transfer to the bowl of shrimp.

Add the avocado just before serving. Serve with saltines or tortilla chips, additional hot sauce, and lime wedges.

COCTEL *de* CAMARÓN

SALADS
Ensaladas

We've all seen roasted beets paired with blue cheese and we all love it. What's special about this salad is the macha caramelized pecans. Once you learn to make them, you can use them to uplift any salad.

Roasting a beet is a straightforward and simple process that many people shy away from, but a roasted beet is a great ingredient to have on hand to throw into all kinds of salads and to use as a side dish. *Serves 4*

4 medium beets, trimmed and wrapped in aluminum foil

1 fennel bulb, core removed, thinly sliced, fronds optionally reserved and chopped

1 cup pomegranate seeds

1 large shallot, thinly sliced

2 cups shredded kale

3½ ounces ounces blue cheese, crumbled, divided

DRESSING

¼ cup extra-virgin olive oil

3 tablespoons red wine vinegar

1 teaspoon honey

1 teaspoon Dijon mustard

Flaky sea salt and freshly ground pepper

Macha Pecans (optional)

Preheat the oven to 400°F. Roast the beets in aluminum foil until tender when pierced with a knife, about 1 hour.

While the beets roast, make the dressing: Whisk together the olive oil, vinegar, honey, and Dijon in a small bowl. Season with salt and pepper to taste.

When cool enough to handle, peel the beets, cut into wedges, and place in a large bowl.

Add the fennel, pomegranate seeds, shallot, kale, and most of the cheese to the beets. Add the dressing and toss, garnish with the remaining cheese, and top with the macha pecans, if desired.

MACHA PECANS

These are superaddictive. That's the feedback I get from everyone who cooks this. You are going to make these and have to control yourself before you put them on the salad because the sweet, savory, smoky, spicy combo is like candy. *Makes 1½ cups*

1½ cups pecan halves

3 tablespoons honey

2 tablespoons salsa macha, mostly the solid pieces (drained of too much oil)

⅛ teaspoon ground cumin

½ teaspoon garlic powder

Preheat the oven to 400°F. Line a rimmed baking sheet with a silicone mat. Toss together all the ingredients in a medium bowl and spread in a single layer on the prepared baking sheet. Bake until browned, about 10 minutes. Remove from the oven, let cool slightly, and break apart. Store in an airtight container at room temperature.

WEDGE SALAD *with Blue Cheese and Chipotle Caramelized Pecans*

Here we go with the caramelized pecans again! The wedge salad is a personal obsession and I needed to include a recipe for it because I love it so much. When I was pregnant with my kids, we would go to Morton's Steakhouse just to get a wedge salad, and that's why it's in this book. There's nothing special except for the chipotle and the caramelized pecans. It's just straightforward and delicious. I use a 4-ounce package of blue cheese for this, and crumble the remaining ounce not used in the dressing over the finished salad. *Serves 2 to 4*

BLUE CHEESE DRESSING

3 ounces blue cheese, crumbled

3 tablespoons buttermilk

3 tablespoons sour cream

2 tablespoons mayonnaise

1 tablespoon apple cider vinegar

Pinch of garlic powder

Pinch of flaky sea salt

CARAMELIZED PECANS

⅓ cup brown sugar

2 tablespoons water

Zest of 1 lime

1 teaspoon flaky sea salt

1 teaspoon chipotle powder

½ teaspoon garlic powder

½ teaspoon vanilla extract

1½ cups pecan halves

SALAD

1 head iceberg lettuce, outer leaves removed, cut into 4 wedges

1 Bosc pear, cored and thinly sliced

4 slices bacon, cooked and chopped

¼ cup chopped fresh parsley

½ cup cherry tomato halves

1 ounce blue cheese, crumbled (optional)

To make the dressing, place the 3 ounces of blue cheese in a medium bowl, and mash with the back of a fork. Stir in the buttermilk, sour cream, mayonnaise, vinegar, garlic powder, and salt. Set aside. Made one day ahead, the flavors intensify!

Caramelize the pecans: Line a large rimmed baking sheet with a silicone mat or heavily greased waxed paper. Combine the brown sugar, water, lime zest, salt, chipotle powder, garlic powder, and vanilla in a medium nonstick skillet over medium heat. Stir with a heat-resistant rubber spatula to dissolve the sugar. Continue to stir, and when the mixture bubbles, stir in the pecans. Continue to cook, stirring frequently to not burn the pecans, until shiny and coated, about 4 minutes. Transfer to the prepared baking sheet and spread out with a spatula. Let cool.

To assemble the salad, place the lettuce wedges on a platter and arrange the pear slices around the wedges. Top with the blue cheese dressing. Garnish with the bacon, parsley, and cherry tomato halves. Scatter the pecan halves over the salad. You'll have some left over to snack on. Crumble additional blue cheese on top (if using), and serve.

Nopales, or cactus paddles, are packed with fiber and nutrients, and are now very easy to find at the supermarket. If you don't have access to them, you can substitute three-quarters of a head of shredded cabbage for an equally delicious and healthy slaw.

The trickiest, or most potentially off-putting, part of cactus paddles is the slime they release when cooking. In this recipe, I cook them in a nontraditional way, without boiling them—no liquid added. Because I don't add any water, the cactus paddles release their juices, which then evaporate while cooking, so they lose a lot of that slimy texture. Immediately rinsing them after cooking also gives you a cleaner nopal.

If you have any left over, throw them in your morning smoothie, uncooked, and you won't even taste them. *Serves 4*

1½ pounds cactus paddles with spikes removed (they can be purchased this way), thinly sliced into ¼-inch-thick strips

½ medium white onion, unsliced, plus ½ medium white onion, thinly sliced (about ½ cup)

3 bay leaves

Pinch of dried oregano

Flaky sea salt

2 Roma tomatoes, seeded and diced

½ cauliflower, sliced into broad ⅛- to ¼-inch slices

Serrano-Avocado Dressing (recipe follows)

¼ cup toasted, salted pepitas

4 radishes, quartered

Everything bagel seasoning with chipotle flakes (optional)

Place the sliced cactus paddles in a large, heavy pot along with the unsliced onion half, bay leaves, pinch of oregano, and a large pinch of salt. Cook over medium heat, stirring frequently, until the cactus turns olive green and the liquid has evaporated. Drain the cactus and rinse with cold water. Discard the onion and bay leaf. Pat the cactus very dry and transfer to a bowl.

Mix in the tomatoes, thinly sliced onion, and cauliflower, being careful not to break the cauliflower pieces too much. Carefully fold in the dressing and pepitas. Transfer to a platter. Top with the quartered radishes and bagel seasoning, if desired. Serve.

ENSALADA *de* NOPALES

SERRANO-AVOCADO DRESSING

This dressing will work with any salad, but if you use it with tender greens, you may want to thin it out a bit. It will be beautiful with any tossed salad, like a potato salad or pasta salad—ingredients that can take a heartier dressing. *Makes 1¼ cups dressing*

½ cup loosely packed fresh cilantro leaves

1 fresh serrano chile, stemmed and seeded (use half if you don't want the heat!)

½ medium avocado, pitted and peeled

2 tablespoons extra-virgin olive oil

Juice of ½ lemon

Flaky sea salt and freshly ground black pepper

1 to 2 tablespoons water

In a high-powered blender, blend together the cilantro, serrano, avocado, olive oil, and lemon juice until very smooth. Season to taste with salt and black pepper. Add water as necessary. The dressing should not be too stiff!

I grew up eating hearts of palm from a can with salt and saltine crackers. The hearts of palm make this substantial salad a bit lighter, but you can skip them altogether and just make this a potato salad. It's truly delicious and great for the summer—unexpected but familiar all at the same time. ***Serves 6***

1½ pounds Yukon Gold potatoes, peeled

1 fresh jalapeño chile

2 cups chopped tomatoes with no seeds (from about 4 medium vine-ripened tomatoes)

3 tablespoons chopped fresh mint

3 tablespoons chopped fresh fennel fronds (optional)

½ medium white onion, chopped (½ cup)

1 fresh serrano chile, stemmed, seeded, and minced

2 14-ounce jars hearts of palm, well drained and coarsely chopped

¾ cup Mex-Italian Dressing (recipe follows)

Flaky sea salt and freshly ground black pepper

Place the potatoes and jalapeño in a large pot and cover with 3 inches of water. Add 1 tablespoon of salt and bring to a boil over high heat. Boil until tender, about 20 minutes. Drain and place under cold running water to cool. Discard the jalapeño.

Cut the potatoes in half or into quarters. Transfer to a large bowl and gently mix in the remaining ingredients, except the salt and black pepper. Let stand at room temperature for 30 minutes to 2 hours to blend the flavors. Add salt and black pepper to taste, if necessary.

MEX-ITALIAN DRESSING

You don't have to make this in a molcajete, but if you have one, please use it. The magic of the pre-Hispanic tool is its ability to extract oils in a way that the blades of the processor can't. Flavors are deeper and richer, and texture is superior as well. It will be delicious no matter what, but there's a reason this tool has stood the test of time for *thousands* of years: it works. ***Make 1½ cups***

5 garlic cloves, unpeeled

2 dried guajillo chiles, stems and seeds removed

½ teaspoon black peppercorns

½ teaspoon coriander seeds

Flaky sea salt

1 teaspoon garlic powder

1 teaspoon dried oregano

1 teaspoon dried parsley

1 teaspoon dried basil

1 teaspoon onion powder

1 cup extra-virgin olive oil

½ cup red wine vinegar

Freshly ground black pepper

Heat a comal or large cast-iron skillet over very high heat. Add the unpeeled garlic and toast until blackened, about 5 minutes. Add the guajillos, peppercorns, and coriander seeds and toast until fragrant, about 2 minutes, moving them constantly.

Peel the garlic and place in a molcajete. Add 1 teaspoon of salt and mash to a paste. It will seem like it's all stuck to the walls of the molcajete, but that's okay! Add the toasted peppercorns and coriander, then mash. Add the toasted chiles and mash them against the walls of the molcajete until disintegrated. Add all the remaining ingredients, except the olive oil, vinegar, and black pepper, and mash into the paste.

Add ⅓ cup of the olive oil and stir/mash to slowly create a dressing. Gradually add the remaining oil. Scrape into a bowl and whisk in the vinegar. Season to taste with additional salt and black pepper.

This is an absolute staple at my house. If you follow me on social media, you know that the kids and I eat this at least two or three times a week. It's easy to put together and works year-round. This recipe comes from my mother-in-law, Philip's mom, and it was her idea to add a splash of raspberry vinaigrette to add a hint of tart sweetness to the dressing.

In Mexico, the cucumbers have a thicker, smoother, shinier skin that is completely edible and often left on to add texture to the dish. *Serves 4*

3 hothouse cucumbers, unpeeled (if organic), thinly sliced

⅓ cup good extra-virgin olive oil

⅓ cup red wine vinegar

1 to 2 tablespoons prepared raspberry vinaigrette (optional)

⅓ cup chopped fresh mint

½ red onion, thinly sliced (about 1 cup)

Tons of flaky sea salt and freshly ground black pepper

Toss together all the ingredients in a large bowl. Let stand for 30 minutes at room temperature. Eat.

GRILLED ROMAINE SALAD

Tijuana is the birthplace of the Caesar salad. Here, we're breaking away from tradition by grilling the romaine to add more layers of flavor and to get that charred component, as opposed to the classic version tossed in a giant wooden bowl, tableside, in downtown TJ. *Serves 4*

CAESAR DRESSING

2 garlic cloves, minced

1 tablespoon capers

1 anchovy filet

2 tablespoons mayonnaise

2 tablespoons Worcestershire sauce

1 tablespoon freshly squeezed lemon juice

1 tablespoon Dijon mustard

1 teaspoon red wine vinegar

½ cup extra-virgin olive oil

⅓ cup freshly grated Parmesan cheese

Flaky sea salt and freshly ground black pepper

ROMAINE SALAD

Extra-virgin olive oil

2 hearts romaine lettuce, cut in half lengthwise

Flaky sea salt and freshly ground black pepper

3 1-inch-thick slices rustic bread

1 tablespoon granulated sugar

2 lemons, halved

Preheat your grill or grill pan to medium-high heat.

Make the dressing: In your molcajete, combine the garlic, capers, and anchovy and mash until you have a thick, homogeneous paste.

In a small bowl, combine the mayonnaise, Worcestershire sauce, lemon juice, Dijon mustard, vinegar, and molcajete paste. Slowly whisk in the olive oil. Add the Parmesan cheese and continue to whisk. Season with salt and pepper to taste.

To make the salad, drizzle olive oil on the cut romaine hearts and season with salt and pepper. Place the romaine, cut side down, on the grill and cook until it has nice grilling marks, about 3 minutes. Brush the bread slices with olive oil and place on the grill. Cook until you have grill marks on both sides and the bread is crispy, about 5 minutes.

Spread out the sugar on a small plate. Dip the cut sides of the lemons into the sugar, then grill the lemon halves until slightly charred and grill marked, 4 to 5 minutes.

Cut the bread into bite-size croutons. Place the romaine hearts, croutons, and lemons on a wooden board and serve with your Caesar dressing.

TRADITIONAL FLAVORS
Sabores Tradicionales

Cochinita pibil is a traditional dish from the Yucatán. There are so many stories to tell about it. The first time I tried this dish, it was made by a man named Pedro who lived and cooked with us throughout my childhood because my mom was sick and didn't cook much. It wasn't until a recent trip to Mérida that I ate it again, after twenty years.

Obviously we're bypassing tradition by not digging a pit in the backyard, but whether you're burying your pork underground or doing it in the oven, the key to this dish is simplicity. The success is in the subtle flavor of the achiote; you must fully cook out the flavor of the raw annatto seeds to get a mellow, tender shredded pork without any overwhelming flavors. *Serves 6 to 8*

½ cup freshly squeezed orange juice

½ cup freshly squeezed grapefruit juice

¼ cup apple cider vinegar

½ 1.75-ounce achiote bar

½ medium white onion

2 garlic cloves, peeled

2 tablespoons flaky sea salt

2 teaspoons ground cumin

2 teaspoons dried oregano

1½ pounds boneless pork shoulder, cut into 1½-inch chunks

2 large banana leaves (thawed, if frozen)

Pickled White Onions with Habanero (recipe follows), for serving

Preheat the oven to 375°F. Combine the orange juice, grapefruit juice, cider vinegar, achiote, onion, garlic, salt, cumin, and oregano in a blender and blend until fully incorporated. Place the chunks of meat in a large bowl, add the blended mixture, cover, and marinate for 30 minutes.

For pliable banana leaves, quickly graze them over a gas burner or grill turned to medium to high heat; they will turn a softer olive green. Line a shallow baking dish with pliable banana leaves, placing them in a cross that is large enough to cover its interior and hang over the sides.

Transfer the marinated meat and its marinade to your baking dish over the banana leaves and cover with the overhanging portion of the crossed banana leaves, to enclose the meat. Cover the baking dish with aluminum foil and bake for about 1 hour. Then, remove from the oven and shred the pork with a fork. Spoon any sauce over the cochinita and serve with the pickled onions.

COCHINITA PIBIL *al* HORNO

PICKLED WHITE ONIONS WITH HABANERO

My sincere apologies to the woman in class who had a conniption over me using white onions here instead of the traditional red ones. I made it with white onions because I ran out of red, but I really appreciated the crispness of the white onion with the habanero. In this case, it really worked to break away from tradition. *Serves 8 to 10*

1 medium white onion, thinly sliced

1 habanero chile, thinly sliced

1 cup distilled white vinegar

1 tablespoon dried oregano

2 bay leaves

¼ cup extra-virgin olive oil

Juice of 1 lime

Flaky sea salt

Mix together all the ingredients in a shallow bowl. Store in an airtight container in the fridge for up to 3 days.

A sope is like a tostada with raised edges that's more chewy than crisp. This recipe is for making the actual "sope," the vehicle that will carry all the deliciousness. In terms of what you put in it, it could just be the smashed beans that follow and a sprinkle of queso fresco, a drizzle of salsa, and then some lettuce. It's a great way to use any leftover protein like shredded chicken, chorizo, or beef. Even carne asada! Once you add shredded lettuce and salsa, pretty much anything tastes amazing. And I understand if you just want to top your sopes with supermarket hot sauce. That's good, too; sopes are a dish that's all about just using up what you have. *Makes about 8 sopes*

2 cups masa harina

1½ to 2 cups hot water

Extra-virgin olive oil, for the baking sheet

FOR SERVING

Frijoles Machacados (recipe follows)

Boiled Chile de Árbol Salsa (page 203) or another favorite

Crema Mexicana

Avocado slices

Shredded iceberg lettuce dressed with a little olive oil, vinegar, salt, and black pepper

Queso fresco

Preheat the oven to 400°F. In a large bowl, mix the masa harina and 1½ cups of the hot water. Add more water, little by little, until the masa doesn't crack when rolled. Mix the masa with your hand for about 2 minutes to fully combine. It should feel like Play-Doh (sprinkle with a little water if it's still cracking after 2 minutes). Cover with a clean, wet cloth or napkin and let stand for 20 minutes.

Heat a comal or cast-iron griddle over medium heat. Shape the masa into 1½-inch balls (they are called testales at this stage!). Using a tortilla press lined with plastic wrap, or a rolling pin, roll each dough ball into a disk slightly thicker than a tortilla. Working with two or three at a time, transfer to the hot comal, and cook for 30 seconds. Flip and cook for 1 minute. Flip once more and cook until the masa is done and looks opaque (not raw) all over. Remove from the comal and let cool slightly.

While a tortilla is still warm, pinch it outward, using your thumb, to create a raised edge. If it's too hot to handle, cover the tortilla with a piece of plastic wrap so you won't burn yourself. Transfer the sopes to a rimmed baking sheet and brush with a little olive oil. Bake for 10 minutes, or until golden brown.

To serve, spread some frijoles machacados on the bottom center of each sope. Then, simply top with all the additional garnishes!

FRIJOLES MACHACADOS

Frijoles machacados (smashed beans) are a version of refried beans that are much lighter on the fat than the traditional dish, which uses lard. Instead, these use a little butter and olive oil. But if you don't want to make frijoles de la olla and then the machacados because they take forever, I get it. I'm not going to tell anybody if you substitute a can of refried beans for your sopes. ***Makes about 2 cups***

1 tablespoon unsalted butter

1 tablespoon extra-virgin olive oil

1 whole fresh serrano chile

2 garlic cloves, minced

2 teaspoons dehydrated onion

2 cups cooked Frijoles de la Olla (recipe follows), drained, reserving all liquid, or 1 15-ounce can pinto beans, preferably organic, drained (optionally reserving their liquid) and rinsed

¼ cup low-sodium chicken broth, or liquid from the beans, plus more if desired

Flaky sea salt and freshly ground black pepper

Melt the butter with the olive oil in a large saucepan over medium-high heat. Add the serrano, garlic, and dehydrated onion and cook until the chile begins to brown, about 1 minute. Add the beans and chicken broth. Cook over medium heat, frequently mashing only the beans until they become a paste, about 10 minutes. Add more chicken broth or bean cooking liquid, if desired. Season with salt and black pepper to taste. Remove and discard the chile, and serve.

FRIJOLES DE LA OLLA

Frijoles de la olla is a base recipe for Mexican cuisine, and you must learn to make this to consider yourself any sort of Mexican cook. They are the base for refried beans or frijoles machacados.

There are so many different things you can do with frijoles de la olla, including serve them just as they are, in a soup bowl, with traditional garnishes: crema Mexicana, cilantro, chopped white onion, a ton of flaky sea salt, and if you ask my mom, a drizzle of olive oil. *Makes about 6 cups of beans*

2 cups dried pinto beans, soaked for at least 3 hours or overnight in plenty of water

4 garlic cloves, peeled and smashed

¼ large white onion

2 bay leaves

Flaky sea salt and freshly ground black pepper

Combine the drained beans, garlic, onion, and bay leaves in a medium pot. Add 8 cups of water. Do not add salt to the water! Bring to a boil over medium-high heat. Lower the heat to medium-low, cover, and simmer until the beans are tender, about 2 hours. Add more HOT water if the beans are absorbing too much liquid. The beans should be soupy when done, with plenty of liquid remaining. Season the cooked beans with salt and pepper to taste.

The beans can be prepared 5 days ahead. Let cool, cover, and refrigerate. Bring to a boil to reheat before serving.

SOPES CON FRIJOLES

This feeds some people, so call the neighbors unless they're weirdos. Maybe call your sister. And before you have a meltdown because I added bacon to this recipe, let me explain. The reason street tacos al pastor are tender and juicy and fabulous is that they spend *hours* on that vertical spit. We don't have that luxury; the bacon gives us that much-needed fat and lubrication, and basically disappears in the layers.

We're stealing this technique from the smart taqueros across Mexico, who know that pineapple enzymes tenderize meat, so they interleave the slices of pineapple with pork on their spits. We're doing the same thing in our ovens. As for the pork, you *must* pound it into thin, milanesa-style pieces. Don't worry if it's not perfect. You just need to be able to make layers. And get *thin* slices on that pineapple too! **Serves 10 to 12**

2 dried guajillo chiles, soaked in warm water for 10 minutes, then drained

2 dried ancho chiles, soaked in warm water for 10 minutes, then drained

2 garlic cloves, peeled

1¾ ounces achiote paste (half of a 3.5-ounce bar)

¼ cup distilled white vinegar

½ cup orange soda

Flaky sea salt and freshly ground black pepper

1½ pounds boneless pork shoulder, sliced into ½-inch-thick slices (Milanese-style)

¼ cup canola oil, plus more for the pan

10 slices uncooked bacon

½ small pineapple, peeled, cored, and cut into ¼-inch-thick slices

Small corn tortillas

½ medium white onion, finely chopped (about ½ cup)

½ cup finely chopped fresh cilantro

4 limes, quartered

Fresh salsa (optional)

In a blender, combine the rehydrated guajillos and anchos, garlic cloves, achiote paste, vinegar, soda, and a pinch of salt and black pepper. Blend until everything is combined; the consistency should be pastelike. Set this adobo paste aside.

Place a slice of meat between two sheets of plastic wrap. Using a meat mallet or rolling pin, gently flatten the meat until it is very thin, about ¼ inch thick. Continue with the remaining meat.

Oil a rimmed baking sheet. This will help your meat to not stick to the pan. Start by putting a couple of slices of meat on the pan. Season with salt and black pepper. Spread some of the adobo paste on the meat until fully covered, top with 3 slices of the bacon, and then with a few pineapple slices. Repeat until you have layered all the meat, bacon, and pineapple into a compact rectangular stack.

Preheat the oven to 375°F. Let the pan sit at room temperature for 15 minutes (so it's not too cold when you put it in the oven). Drizzle with the ¼ cup of oil and roast until cooked through in the center, 40 to 50 minutes.

Remove from the oven, let sit for 10 minutes, then transfer the entire stack of meat to a cutting board (do not discard the oil left on the baking pan; it will be used to heat the tortillas). Starting from an edge of the stack, thinly slice downward to get a stack of thinly sliced, cooked strips of pork and pineapple. Cut several more slices the same way, so you can make a few tacos.

Once your meat is sliced, using a pastry brush, smear leftover oil from the pan on both sides of each tortilla you plan to serve. Place a dry skillet over medium-high heat and heat the tortillas, one by one, until warmed through.

Make tacos with the sliced meat, onion, cilantro, and a sprinkle of lime juice. Go ahead and add fresh salsa (if you have any), but I think this has enough flavor as is!

I found chiles en nogada off-putting as a child because of the texture of the sauce. Depending who makes it, the traditional nut-based sauce can be really grainy. That's why I'm constantly talking about how to make it supersmooth.

Chiles en nogada also contain surprising combination of flavors, if you're tasting the dish as a person who did not grow up in the Mexican culture. Here you're getting sweet, sour, savory, creamy, plus a little smoky. It's unexpected if you're expecting a stereotypical Mexican plate.

As beautifully explained by the late master Yuri de Gortari, one of the most knowledgeable humans in Mexican food, traditional chiles en nogada are coated and deep-fried. This dish, born in the Virreinato (Viceroyalty of New Spain), carried with it some European culinary techniques, like whipping eggs and using them to coat foods for frying. So, if you coated, stuffed, and fried something, it was almost a status symbol. Thighs be damned. But I like my chiles uncoated and my thighs tiny. (Seriously, you can do either—and my Chiles Rellenos, page 72, are fried.)

I use cashews here instead of the traditional walnuts, because I once peeled so many walnuts for an event that I vowed never to do it again. (Because of the grooves in the walnuts, I had to use tweezers to get every last piece of skin. They get under your nails. Bless you if you want to do that.)

To char the tomatoes, place them in a dry pan (no oil), preferably cast iron, and cook for about 12 minutes, turning occasionally, until charred on all sides. When cool enough to handle, peel and transfer to a blender and blend on high speed until very smooth. Char the poblanos separately and do not puree.

Finally, serving temperature is key here. Not cold, not hot, but right in the middle, like Mexican Goldilocks. Serve this the moment you make it. *Serves 6 to 8*

2 tablespoons good-quality lard or vegetable oil

½ medium white onion, chopped (about ½ cup)

4 garlic cloves, minced

1 pound ground meat (beef or a combo of beef and pork)

3 Roma tomatoes, charred, peeled, and pureed in a blender until smooth

¼ cup raisins

¼ cup candied pineapple pieces (small pieces)

¼ cup dried apricot pieces (small pieces)

1 teaspoon ground cinnamon

¼ teaspoon ground cloves

¼ cup slivered almonds

1 pear, unpeeled, stemmed, seeded, and diced

1 red apple, unpeeled, stemmed, seeded, and diced

Flaky sea salt and freshly ground black pepper

6 to 8 fresh poblano chiles, charred, peeled, and slit, seeds removed, for stuffing

Cashew Nogada Sauce (recipe follows)

½ cup chopped fresh parsley

½ cup pomegranate seeds

Melt the lard in a large, heavy pot over medium-high heat. Add the onion and garlic and sauté for 4 minutes. Add the ground meat and increase the heat to high. Using the back of a wooden spoon, break apart the meat so you have no clumps, and sauté for 3 minutes.

Strain the pureed tomatoes into the same pan and lower the heat slightly. Cook for 2 minutes to incorporate and reduce slightly. Add the raisins, pineapple, apricots, cinnamon, cloves, and almonds and stir well to combine.

Cook for 3 minutes. Add the pear and apple and cook for 5 to 8 minutes longer, or until the fruit is slightly tender. Season well with salt and black pepper to taste.

Generously stuff the poblanos with the meat filling and arrange, slit side down, on a platter. Pour the nogada sauce over the chiles (but not their stems), sprinkle with parsley and pomegranate seeds, and serve JUST warm.

CASHEW NOGADA SAUCE

Pay attention to this cashew sauce. It can be your go-to substitute for dairy, like heavy cream, with a few tweaks like leaving out the sherry and goat cheese (traditional ingredients for nogada). Replace those with a little vinegar and salt, and you have vegan cream that's ridiculously delish!

In this recipe, you will use a combination of cashews and almonds instead of the traditional walnuts. If you wish to use walnuts, simply heat 6 cups of milk to a simmer, remove from the heat, and add the walnuts. Let sit for 4 hours and then peel off all of the thin brown skin. Reserve 1 cup of the milk as the liquid to make the nogada.

Note: You *must* soak the nuts a day ahead. Don't skip that, or you won't get a silky-smooth sauce. And I just cannot handle grainy sauces. ***Makes enough for 8 chiles***

2½ cups raw cashews

½ cup slivered almonds

6 cups water, for soaking

1½ ounces fresh goat cheese

2 tablespoons sherry wine

1 teaspoon sherry vinegar

Flaky sea salt, for seasoning

Granulated sugar, for seasoning

Place the cashews, almonds. and water in a bowl. Cover with plastic wrap or a clean cloth and let sit overnight. Drain, reserving 1 cup of the soaking liquid.

Combine the reserved cup of soaking liquid, soaked nuts, cheese, wine, and vinegar in a blender and blend until VERY smooth. Season to taste with salt and sugar, using anywhere from a pinch to a few tablespoons of sugar depending on how sweet you like the nogada.

CHILES EN NOGADA

These are traditional chilaquiles with a hint of smoky heat from canned chipotles in adobo. If you don't want as much heat, just use the adobo sauce that comes with the chipotles and don't add any actual chile. And, by all means, add more chipotle if you like things really hot.

I like to fry eggs to top the chilaquiles, but both the eggs and the shredded turkey can be left out entirely. You can also have them "naturales" with no protein. Up to you! *Serves 4*

3 tablespoons extra-virgin olive oil

5 Roma tomatoes (about 2¼ pounds), roughly chopped

2 garlic cloves, roughly chopped

¼ medium yellow onion, roughly chopped (about ¼ cup)

1 or 2 canned chipotle chiles in adobo sauce

1 dried guajillo chile, stemmed, seeded, and torn into pieces

Flaky sea salt and freshly ground black pepper

1 cup shredded cooked turkey meat

TORTILLA CHIPS

Vegetable oil

8 6-inch corn tortillas

Flaky sea salt

FOR SERVING

4 large eggs, fried (optional)

Crumbled queso fresco

Thinly sliced red onion

Crema Mexicana

Avocado slices

Chopped fresh cilantro

Heat the olive oil in a medium heavy-bottomed skillet over medium-high heat. Add the tomatoes, garlic, and onion and sauté until golden brown, 10 minutes. Add the chipotles and guajillo pieces and sauté for another minute. Transfer, along with 1 teaspoon of salt and ½ teaspoon of black pepper, to a blender and process until smooth. Return the mixture to the skillet and cook over medium-low heat for 5 minutes. Stir in the shredded turkey and season with additional salt and black pepper. Keep warm.

For the tortilla chips, heat 2 inches of vegetable oil in a large sauté pan until a deep-fry thermometer inserted in the oil registers 375°F. While it's heating, stack the tortillas and cut into quarters, then into quarters again (to make eight equal triangles per tortilla). Working in batches, fry the tortilla triangles until crisp and golden, about 4 minutes. Remove from the oil and drain on a paper towel–lined baking sheet. Season with salt.

Add the tortilla chips to the skillet of warm salsa, making sure all the chips are fully coated with the salsa, then transfer to a serving dish. Top with fried eggs, if desired, and sprinkle with queso fresco. Garnish with red onion, crema Mexicana, avocado, and cilantro.

CHIPOTLE CHILAQUILES

The ultimate comfort food! If you grew up in a home where chiles rellenos were made, the anticipation of it is what's magical. Preparing this dish is a process that takes a while and its scent completely engulfs your home. Coming home from school, I would know what we were having for dinner when I could smell the frying poblanos from the street. For me, this dish is a return home.

These are made across Mexico. In Puebla, the right way to make a chile relleno is to batter and deep-fry it, as in this recipe. Elsewhere, you will find versions of this where the chile is stuffed, sauced, and served without being battered and fried. You can certainly just stuff the chiles with cheese and bake them at 350°F for 25 minutes. I only recommend frying if coating them in this type of batter.

You have other options too. I like using Oaxaca cheese because it doesn't fully melt, staying neatly inside the chile. If you prefer melted cheese to ooze out of the chile, go for a soft Manchego or Monterey Jack. Cut the cheese into rectangles because shredded cheese is harder to keep inside the chile.

When you char the chiles and are ready to peel, have a bowl close by and reserve the charred skin. It is so flavorful! I throw it into a baking pan in the oven at 200°F for a while to dehydrate it. You can mix it into salsas, or with flaky salt for a charred poblano salt that is excellent for finishing any dish. Same for the tomato skins. You can air-fry or deep-fry them and they add so much flavor as a garnish! *Serves 4*

5 Roma tomatoes, cored and scored with a shallow X

3 medium tomatillos, husked and rinsed

6 dried costeño chiles or 4 dried guajillos, stemmed and seeded

3 garlic cloves, peeled and smashed

½ teaspoon dried oregano

1 tablespoon brown sugar

Pinch of baking soda

1 tablespoon extra-virgin olive oil

Flaky sea salt

1 quart vegetable oil, for frying (I use avocado oil)

5 fresh poblano chiles, charred and peeled

8 ounces Oaxaca cheese strings

5 large eggs, at room temperature, separated (you will use only 3 of the yolks)

Pinch of cream of tartar

¼ cup all-purpose flour

Chopped fresh cilantro, for garnish

Bring a medium pot of salted water to a boil over high heat. Add the tomatoes, tomatillos, and chiles, bring back to a boil, and boil for 3 minutes. Turn off the heat and let stand for 10 minutes.

Peel the tomatoes. You can discard the tomato skins, or fry and salt them and add to the dish as garnish. Place the tomatoes, tomatillos, and stemmed chiles in a blender. Add the garlic, oregano, brown sugar, and baking soda. Blend until a very smooth salsa.

Heat the olive oil in a medium, heavy pot over high heat. Add the salsa and cook, stirring occasionally, just until fragrant. Season with salt to taste. Keep over low heat while the chiles are prepared.

Heat the vegetable oil over low heat in a very large sauté pan with high sides.

Clean your poblanos by carefully cutting a slit down the center (make sure the slit cuts only on the top side of each chile, like you're making a purse) and removing the seeds. Be careful while removing the veins, as that can rip the chile. Stuff each with a few pieces of Oaxaca cheese and set aside.

To make the batter, make sure you clean your bowl and your beaters with a little bit of distilled white vinegar to remove any debris or fat. Place all 5 egg whites and the cream of tartar in a large bowl. Whip on high speed until stiff peaks form and the whites don't fall out if you flip the bowl upside down. Sift the flour into the whipped whites and add 3 yolks (reserve the other 2 yolks for another use). Quickly incorporate the flour and egg yolks with an electric mixer on low speed. Do not overmix as you will deflate the batter!

Increase the heat beneath the pot of oil to high. Holding each chile by the stem, and using a spoon to help you pour batter evenly over chile, dip the stuffed chiles in the egg batter and then carefully place in the hot oil. I would fry only two chiles at a time. Fry until golden brown, 6 to 8 minutes per side. Transfer to paper towels to drain but serve immediately.

To serve, place the salsa on a plate and top with the chiles. You can garnish with charred poblano bits, fried tomato skins, and fresh cilantro, or these ingredients can be mixed into the salsa before serving.

GAME CHANGER

@megs.urban.garden

When making chile rellenos, I learned how to cut a chile poblano to secure the cheese filling, without having to use a toothpick; I learned how to get the perfect puff when making handmade tortillas; brushing sopes with a little olive oil and baking them, rather than deep frying, has definitely been a game changer; lastly, adding shredded iceberg lettuce dressed with a little olive oil, vinegar, salt & pepper to tostadas, sopes and tacos adds another layer of flavor and is so quick & easy to put together.

CHILES RELLENOS

GAME CHANGER

@sotona1283

One HUGE tip you gave us was to not remove ALL the char from the poblanos and that made a world of difference in the taste.

I love this recipe because I grew up eating it in the iconic Tijuana restaurant, Los Arcos. It's a simple dish that was born in Mazatlán, Sinaloa, Mexico, a state famous for its creative shrimp preparations, and named after the governor to whom it was first served, Francisco Labastida. You get a surprising combo that you may not see anywhere else: shrimp, poblanos, and melted cheese. They work beautifully together. Don't be confused by the name: they're called tacos, but they're like a fried quesadilla with shrimp. *Makes 6 to 8 tacos*

2 tablespoons extra-virgin olive oil

½ medium white onion, diced (about ½ cup)

3 garlic cloves, minced

2 fresh poblano chiles, charred, peeled, seeded, and diced

2½ pounds raw shrimp, peeled, deveined, and chopped into large chunks (about 2 cups; I like 16/20 shrimp, but any size will work)

Flaky sea salt and freshly ground black pepper

Olive oil, to cook the tortillas

6 to 8 tortillas

2 cups shredded Monterey Jack cheese

Hot sauce and lime, for serving

Heat the extra-virgin olive oil in a large, heavy sauté pan over high heat. Add the onion and sauté for 4 minutes. Add the garlic and sauté for 1 minute longer. Add the poblanos and sauté for just 1 minute longer to combine the flavors. Add the shrimp and stir until they are cooked through, about 4 minutes total. Season the shrimp mixture to taste with salt and black pepper.

To make the tacos, heat a little olive oil in another large, heavy sauté pan. Add 2 tortillas and cook for 30 seconds. Add ¼ cup of the cheese to half of each tortilla and scoop some of the shrimp mixture over it.

Fold the other half of the tortilla over the shrimp and cheese, and cook until the cheese at the edge is crusty. Repeat, working in batches and adding more oil if needed, until all the tacos are made. Serve with hot sauce and lime!

TACOS GOBERNADOR

MULITAS *de* CARNE ASADA

Mulitas are like the elevated cousin of the street taco: a stacked quesadilla stuffed with carne asada and all the traditional taco toppings. You're guaranteed to make a mess of yourself and the mulita while eating it, but that's the best part.

If you can, start this six hours ahead and get that marinade flavor to really sink into the meat. The paprika adds some heat, so leave it out if you just want flavorful carne asada. My kids David and Anna were seriously upset that they couldn't get past two bites. They tried so hard! *Serves 6 to 8*

3 pounds thinly sliced arrachera or asada meat (flank or carne asada)

¼ cup extra-virgin olive oil

Juice of 2 tangerines

5 ounces lager beer

1 tablespoon flaky sea salt

1 teaspoon freshly ground black pepper, or less if desired

1 teaspoon paprika (skip if your kids don't like spice)

1 medium white onion, thinly sliced (about 1 cup)

2 tangerines, unpeeled, thinly sliced

Oil, for the grill

FOR ASSEMBLY

12 to 16 corn tortillas

4 cups shredded white melting cheese (Monterey Jack, queso quesadilla, mozzarella)

Salsa Taquera de Chile Morita (page 215)

Salsa de Guacamole (recipe follows)

Chopped fresh cilantro

Minced white onion

Lime wedges

Place the meat in a large dish, such as Pyrex. Add the oil, tangerine juice, beer, salt, pepper, and paprika (if using), and really massage them into the meat. Place the onion and tangerine slices in between the meat layers. Cover with plastic wrap and refrigerate for least 1 hour or up to 6 hours.

Bring the meat to room temperature 30 minutes before cooking. Pat the meat dry before grilling it. Discard the juice mixture. I like to sauté and serve the onion and tangerine slices, but you can discard them.

Heat a grill pan over high heat and brush lightly with oil. Working in batches, add only two pieces of meat at a time; do not overlap! Cook until just cooked through, about 4 minutes per side depending on thickness and desired doneness. Transfer to a cutting board and tent with foil. Chop into small pieces.

Wipe the grill pan clean with a paper towel. Add a tortilla and top with a heaping ¼ to ½ cup of the cheese. Scatter some grilled meat over the cheese and top with a second tortilla. Cook until the cheese is melted. You want to watch the mulita so that the tortilla doesn't toast. Sometimes, covering the pan to trap heat and create a little steam helps melt the cheese faster without overdrying the tortilla.

To serve, peel back the upper tortilla and top with all the garnishes.

SALSA DE GUACAMOLE

This is a runny guacamole. It is also what will take your mulita to authentic street taco level. Versus a chunky guac, this is smooth, creamy, and a little spicy. You can add more or less liquid, depending on the texture you want, but you definitely want to add enough so you can pour it, not plop it, on the mulita. If you have any other greens on hand, you can add things like arugula or spinach or even kale, for extra nutrients. ***Makes about 2 cups***

1 or 2 fresh serrano chiles, stemmed and seeded

8 medium tomatillos, husked and rinsed

2 garlic cloves, peeled

½ medium white onion

¼ cup whole milk

1 bunch cilantro, stems removed

2 medium avocados, pitted and peeled

1 tablespoon or more distilled white vinegar

Flaky sea salt

Bring a saucepan of salted water to a boil over high heat. Add the serrano first and cook for 4 minutes. Then, add the tomatillos, garlic, and onion and boil for 3 minutes longer. Drain and transfer to a blender along with the milk, cilantro, avocado, and vinegar. Work in batches if necessary. Blend until very smooth. Season to taste with salt.

Most people don't know that many of our most iconic Mexican dishes have Spanish or European origins. This is one of them, as you can tell from the Basque name "Vizcaina," for the bay between northern Spain and western France. In Spain, the tradition is to eat it on Good Friday and Christmas, and that carried over to Mexico. To me, the flavor profile is reminiscent of an Italian puttanesca because of the combination of the briny olives and the low-and-slow-cooked tomatoes.

This one is a labor of love. It's not difficult at all, but the shredding of the cod is time consuming. Everything else is just chopping and then being close to the stove while it cooks. We get the bacalao, or salt cod, in the Italian market; I buy a whole side of cod and break it down into smaller pieces so they would fit into a bowl to soak in water. Bacalao comes in sides of 1 to 2 pounds each. Both amounts will work with the recipe; less cod just means more tomato sauce!

Find the crustiest French bread for serving, or stick with tradition and find torta (Mexican sandwich) bread (bolillo or telera) at your Mexican bakery. *Serves 12 to 14*

Scan this QR code to see a post on Instagram where I break down some of the prep with photos and video of the shredding:

1 side of bacalao (salt cod), about 1½ pounds

1½ cups extra-virgin olive oil, divided (will be added at different times, so keep an eye out)

1 large white onion, chopped (about 1½ cups)

4 large garlic cloves, minced

5 medium vine-ripened tomatoes (about 1½ pounds), chopped, without seeds

2 28-ounce cans whole peeled San Marzano tomatoes blended with ½ white onion (this is your tomato puree)

¾ teaspoon freshly ground black pepper

4 russet potatoes (about 2½ pounds), peeled, cut into 1½-inch cubes, and soaked in water until needed (this will remove any excess starch)

1 cup chopped fresh parsley

2 8- to 10-ounce cans or jars green olives stuffed with pimientos or sardines

⅓ cup drained capers

Flaky sea salt

Crusty bread, for serving

Cut the bacalao into two or three large pieces, rinse, and then soak, submerged in water, in a large, nonreactive vessel (such as Pyrex) for 3 days. Drain and discard the water three times a day, refilling with fresh water. Keep refrigerated the whole time.

Recipe continues

First, you will shred the bacalao. Rinse it well and pat dry. Shred it the same way you would cooked chicken, but in much smaller, stringier pieces. The tougher parts are cartilage that needs to be discarded. I like to rub the pieces between my fingers to really break it up. Large pieces are hard to chew on, so the finer the shred, the better your bacalao!

Heat ½ cup of the olive oil in a large (like really large), heavy pot over medium heat. Add the onion and sauté until slightly softened, about 8 minutes. Add the garlic and sauté for 3 minutes, stirring frequently. Add the bacalao and ½ cup more olive oil and stir well to combine. Cook, stirring occasionally, until juices are released, about 10 minutes.

Add the chopped fresh tomatoes (not the puree) and ¼ cup of the olive oil, and stir to combine. Add *half* of the tomato puree and bring to a low simmer. Simmer gently for 20 minutes. Season generously with pepper.

Drain the potatoes, then stir them into the mixture along with the parsley and remaining ¼ cup of olive oil, and bring to a boil over high heat. Lower the heat to medium-low and simmer for 1 hour.

Add the remaining tomato puree and the stuffed olives and cook over very low heat, stirring occasionally, until the potatoes are tender and the stew is thick, 2 to 2½ hours. Stir in the capers. Season with salt.

SHREDDED MOLE CHICKEN TACOS

This recipe shows you how to get a delicious, authentic mole with a few unnoticeable shortcuts from the traditional method. You can do whatever you want with this mole, like serve it with boiled chicken the traditional way, turn it into enchiladas or chilaquiles, or make these tacos.

Traditional mole is very labor intensive and calls for you to use a molcajete. We use a blender instead, and that's perfectly fine. Your mole is still going to taste authentic. While I love using a molcajete for salsas, I am more forgiving in this recipe because I don't want you to stand there for three hours grinding nuts and seeds (but you can do that if you want). There is also such an explosion of so many flavors that it's completely forgivable. Another way to save time is to use purchased cooked chicken instead of boiling it from scratch. Rotisserie chicken is totally fine.

Because of the nuts and seeds, you need a *powerful* blender, like a Vitamix. I've destroyed at least two blenders while making this mole, one of them in which the blender exploded all over my top during a live cooking class with about a thousand people watching.

One note about Mexican chocolate: Depending on the brand, it might be literally as hard as a brick and really frustrating to chop with a knife. But there's a trick. While it's still wrapped, grab it with the palm of your hand, and aiming at the center of the disk, bang it with all your might on the corner of a table. It is designed to shatter. That's why it has the wedgelike indentations. *Serves 6 to 8*

ROASTED VEGETABLES

2 Roma tomatoes, halved

1 large white onion, halved

2 large garlic cloves, unpeeled

Extra-virgin olive oil, for drizzling

MOLE

½ cup extra-virgin olive oil

2 ounces dried ancho chile, seeded and deveined

2 ounces dried guajillo chile, seeded and deveined

1 ounce dried pasilla chile, seeded and deveined

4 cups vegetable or chicken broth

SEED MIXTURE

2 tablespoons extra-virgin olive oil

1 stale corn tortilla or just a regular tortilla (don't stress)

1 2-inch piece stale crusty bread (omit for gluten-free version)

⅓ cup unsalted peanuts

⅓ cup pumpkin seeds

⅓ cup sesame seeds

3 tablespoons blanched almonds

2 tablespoons raisins

1 teaspoon dried oregano

½ teaspoon ground cumin

½ teaspoon dried thyme

1 teaspoon coriander seeds

1 teaspoon black peppercorns

1 cinnamon stick

2 medium tomatillos, husked, rinsed, and halved

2 tablespoons extra-virgin
  olive oil

3 tablespoons granulated
  sugar, plus more for
  serving (optional)

½ to 1 disk Mexican
  chocolate, chopped

Flaky sea salt

2 cups shredded cooked
  chicken

FOR ASSEMBLY

About 12 corn tortillas
  (made with no
  preservatives,
  containing only corn
  and slaked lime and
  maybe salt, that would
  be best), or masa for
  tortillas

Avocado oil or any
  vegetable oil, for
  brushing tortillas

Sesame seeds, for garnish

Crema Mexicana, for
  garnish

Chopped fresh cilantro,
  for garnish

Thinly sliced white onion,
  for garnish

Edible flowers, for garnish
  (optional)

To roast the vegetables, preheat the oven to 425°F. Place the tomatoes, onion, and garlic (with peel!) on a rimmed baking sheet. Drizzle lightly with olive oil and roast until the skins are black and blistered and the vegetables softened, about 55 minutes. Remove from the oven and let cool. Once cooled, peel the garlic.

To make the mole, first prepare the broth. In a large, heavy saucepan, heat the ½ cup of olive oil. Fry all the ancho, guajillo, and pasilla in one batch, turning constantly, for about 40 seconds, until fragrant. Transfer to paper towels to drain. Meanwhile, heat 4 cups of the broth to a boil in a separate saucepan over high heat. Once boiling, add the sautéed chiles, lower the heat to medium-low, and simmer for 10 minutes. Remove from the heat and reserve for the next several steps.

In the meantime, to make the seed mixture, heat the olive oil in a large saucepan over medium-high heat, add the tortilla and piece of bread (if using), and cook for 5 minutes, stirring frequently. Add the peanuts, pumpkin seeds, sesame seeds, almonds, raisins, oregano, cumin, thyme, coriander seeds, black peppercorns, and cinnamon stick. Sauté until fragrant and slightly toasted, about 8 minutes. Add the roasted tomatoes, onion, and peeled garlic and sauté for 1 minute to break up the tomatoes. Using a slotted spoon, remove the chiles from the broth, then stir into the seed mixture.

Transfer half of the cooled seed mixture, along with 1 tomatillo, to a high-speed blender. Add 1 cup of the reserved broth and blend for 3 minutes to a very smooth paste, adding more broth, if necessary. Repeat with the remaining seed mixture and tomatillo and another cup of broth. This mixture is the mole.

To make the mole chicken, heat the olive oil in a large, heavy pot over medium-high heat. Add the mole and cook, stirring frequently until darkened, adding more of the reserved broth to your desired consistency. Add the sugar and chocolate. Season with plenty of salt. Here, we will add as much of the remaining broth as needed to get to "enmolada consistency"! When ready to assemble, place 2 cups of the mole in a bowl and stir in the shredded chicken. Season to taste with more salt and sugar.

To assemble, preheat the oven to 350°F. Place the tortillas on a large rimmed baking sheet, trying to overlap as little as possible. Maybe 6 or 8 if it's a larger baking sheet and oven. Brush them on both sides with avocado oil, using a pastry brush. Cook until golden brown but pliable, about 10 minutes.

Working with one warm tortilla at a time, fill the tortilla with some of the mole mixture. Transfer them all to a platter. Top with more mole, if desired, and drizzle with sesame seeds, crema, cilantro, and onion. Edible flowers could be beautiful to finish the dish.

GAME CHANGER

@hey.risha

I learned PATIENCE is the most important ingredient/technique. To be able to be constantly stirring the mole so it doesn't burn, stirring the rice to coat the grains in oil, and leaving the rice to cook without lifting the lid. You can't rush good food.

SHREDDED MOLE CHICKEN TACOS

These are the real deal. Sometimes on the US side of the border, when you think of a burrito, you think of a giant flour tortilla stuffed with rice, beans, lettuce, avocado, chicken, and God knows what else. A real burrito from northern Mexico is slender and filled only with one or two ingredients. Here, we're going with the traditional low-and-slow-braised shredded meat. That's it. All you need other than the tortilla and its shredded beef filling is a salsa to dunk it in between bites. It's the simplicity of this dish that makes it iconic and differentiates it from the American stereotype.

It's important to use the thinnest and most authentic flour tortillas you can find. You should be able to almost see through the best and most authentic flour tortillas.

Makes 12 to 16 burritos

BRAISED BEEF FILLING

2 pounds boneless chuck roast, cut into 3-inch pieces

1 medium carrot

½ medium white onion, unsliced, plus 1 medium white onion, thinly sliced (about 1 cup)

1 large celery rib

2 bay leaves

1 tablespoon extra-virgin olive oil

2 fresh serrano chiles, stemmed, seeded, and minced

1 red bell pepper, stemmed, seeded, and chopped

1 14.5-ounce can diced tomatoes with juice

Flaky sea salt and freshly ground black pepper

BURRITOS

12 to 16 flour tortillas (preferably precocidas)

Extra-virgin olive oil for toasting the rolled burritos

Salsa Taquera (page 214), for serving

To make the beef filling, place the meat, carrot, unsliced onion half, celery, and bay leaves in a large, heavy pot. Add enough water to cover the meat by 4 inches. Bring to a boil over medium heat, lower the heat to medium-low, and simmer until the meat is tender, about 2 hours. Remove from the heat and strain the broth into a bowl, discarding the vegetables and transferring the beef to a plate. Shred the beef.

Rinse the pot, then add the oil and heat over high heat. Add the thinly sliced onion, serrano, and bell pepper and sauté until softened, about 10 minutes. Add the canned tomatoes and sauté for 5 minutes.

Return the beef and 1 cup of the broth to the pot (reserve the remaining broth for another use). Bring to a boil over high heat, lower the heat to medium-low, and simmer, partially covered, until the liquid reduces by about half, about 20 minutes. Season to taste with salt and pepper.

To make the burritos, heat a dry comal or large cast-iron skillet over medium-high heat. Add a tortilla and cook just to warm until it becomes pliable. Transfer to a cutting board. Place about ¼ cup of the filling down the center of the tortilla. Fold the shorter ends over the filling, then roll up like a cigar. Repeat with the remaining filling and tortillas.

Heat your comal or skillet over high heat and oil lightly. Add a burrito, placing the tortilla edge down to seal. Turn on all sides to brown. Repeat with all the burritos. Serve with salsa taquera.

CHICKEN TINGA TOSTADAS

Chicken tinga is a shredded chicken and chipotle dish that originated in Puebla and is popular during the Fiestas Patrias, the celebrations around Mexican Independence Day in September.

This makes A LOT of tinga, around 2 quarts. My family will make this disappear in a day, but if you're cooking for smaller appetites you can cut the recipe in half or freeze the extra! If freezing, make sure you cool it to room temperature first. I suggest you portion it out in three or four small resealable plastic bags and not freeze in one large bag.

You can make the chicken and broth from scratch or you can purchase both.

Serves 8 to 10

SAUCE

6 whole Roma tomatoes, boiled in salted water for 20 minutes (or in chicken broth if you are making broth from scratch)

¼ medium white onion

¼ cup canned chipotles in adobo (use the chiles and the adobo sauce they came with. Add only half of the chiles if you don't want much heat.)

1 cup chicken broth, purchased or homemade (recipe follows)

3 garlic cloves, peeled and halved

Large pinch of flaky sea salt

TINGA

2 tablespoons extra-virgin olive oil

1 medium white onion, thinly sliced

2 garlic cloves, minced

6 cups shredded chicken (from 1 rotisserie chicken or a chicken cooked in homemade broth [recipe follows])

Flaky sea salt and freshly ground black pepper

FOR SERVING

12 to 14 purchased tostadas

2 cups purchased refried beans, warmed (or make from scratch, page 60)

4 cups shredded iceberg lettuce

1 medium avocado, pitted, peeled, and sliced

1 cup crumbled Cotija cheese

Purchased hot sauce (optional)

Crema Mexicana (optional)

Lime wedges

To make the sauce, combine the boiled tomatoes, onion, canned chipotles, chicken broth, halved garlic cloves, and salt in a blender. Blend until very smooth. Set aside.

To make the tinga, heat the olive oil in a large, heavy skillet or wok over high heat. Add the onion and minced garlic and sauté for 5 minutes. Add the chicken and stir to combine. Strain the tomato sauce through a fine-mesh strainer into the pan and stir to combine. Bring to a boil over high heat, lower the heat to medium-low, and simmer to reduce slightly, about 20 minutes. Season the tinga with salt and black pepper to taste.

To serve, place a tostada on a plate. Spread with about 3 tablespoons of refried beans, then top with ⅓ to ½ cup of the tinga. Top with shredded lettuce, then avocado slices, crumbled cheese, and hot sauce and crema, if desired. Serve with lime wedges.

**GAME
CHANGER**

@yoaliciar

Shredding chicken with a mixer is a great hack (see page 92).

_____

@petuuuuuunia

Layered seasoning is key. Oh, and always top with olive oil, flaky sea salt, and pepper!

CHICKEN BROTH

This recipe is totally optional! You need to prepare it ahead if you wish to make the Chicken Tinga Tostadas (page 90) fully from scratch. You will have leftover broth that you can use in a million different ways, or you can freeze it. Use it as a base for soup, to cook your rice or even your pasta. So much flavor and so good for you! *Makes 6 to 8 cups*

2 medium carrots

1 large celery rib

3 bay leaves

1 tablespoon flaky sea salt

½ medium white onion

1 6-pound chicken, cut into 4 to 6 pieces (you can ask your butcher to do this for you)

Fill a large, heavy pot (big enough to fit all the ingredients) with 10 to 12 cups of water. Add all the ingredients, except the chicken pieces, and bring to a boil over high heat. Add the chicken and bring back to a boil. Lower the heat to medium-low and simmer, covered, until the chicken is tender, about 1 hour.

Remove from the heat and let cool for 30 minutes at room temperature. Transfer the chicken pieces to a bowl. Strain the broth, discarding the vegetables.

Remove the skin and bones from the chicken pieces and shred the meat. I like to use a handheld mixer, especially when it's hot—use a very large bowl and low speed so you don't have flying chicken shreds!

This is a great opportunity to show a traditional Mexican dish with a plant-based variation (if you use oil instead of butter and plant-based cheese). It's very filling and very comforting, and perfect for a weeknight meal served with a side salad. It's like a lasagna, but instead of using pasta sheets, you're using tortillas to create those layers.

Serves 4 to 6

12 corn tortillas

Vegetable oil

2 garlic cloves, chopped

1 small white onion, chopped (about ¾ cup)

2 large tomatoes, boiled 30 seconds, peeled, and pureed (about 2 cups)

3 tablespoons unsalted butter or vegetable oil

4½ cups chopped zucchini (from 3 large zucchini)

1½ cups fresh corn kernels (from 1 ear) or thawed frozen

3 poblano chiles, charred, peeled, seeded, deveined, and chopped

½ cup water

Flaky sea salt and freshly ground black pepper

3 cups shredded Oaxaca cheese, or Monterey Jack or other melting cheese

Preheat the oven to 350°F. Evenly scatter the tortillas, slightly overlapping, on a large rimmed baking sheet. Use two baking sheets, if necessary. Brush the tortillas lightly on both sides with vegetable oil. Bake until slightly crisp but still pliable, about 15 minutes. They might get a little foamy while releasing moisture.

Heat 2 tablespoons of vegetable oil in a medium sauté pan over medium heat. Add the garlic and onion and sauté until the onion is translucent, about 3 minutes. Add the tomato puree. Cook for 10 minutes and turn the heat off.

In a separate large sauté pan over medium heat, melt the butter. Add the zucchini and corn. Cook for 2 minutes, then add the chopped poblanos. Add the water to the mixture and cook for 4 more minutes. Season with salt and black pepper to taste.

Oil a 9-by-13-inch or 9-inch square baking pan with 1 tablespoon of vegetable oil. Cover the bottom with about four tortillas. Add ½ cup of the tomato mixture on top of the tortillas. Top with 1½ cups of the zucchini mixture. Add 1 cup of the cheese. Sprinkle with some salt and black pepper. Repeat two more times, tortillas through seasonings, for a total of three layers.

Place the casserole in the oven and bake until the cheese is melted, 10 to 15 minutes. Broil, if desired!

PASTEL AZTECA

PASTEL AZTECA

GAME CHANGER

@cpalmerin

I learned some very basic things that as a daughter of Mexican parents maybe I should have known. Like you just need to boil tomatoes for 30 seconds for the recipe of the pastel Azteca (I would have probably let them go till they looked like they were falling apart).

What makes an entomatada different from an enchilada? Basically, avoiding dried chiles. Even though the salsa is cooked and includes a fresh jalapeño, it's a lighter broth with a stronger tomato flavor than anything else.

These are great as an appetizer if you go for the small tortillas, but are more traditionally a breakfast or lunch dish with a regular-size tortilla. I fill them with queso fresco, but Cotija will work as well. Heck, you can stuff them with shredded chicken or sautéed mushrooms or any filling really that's fully cooked, because it just gets rolled up in the salsa-smothered tortillas and served! *Serves 4 to 6*

6 Roma tomatoes, core removed

¼ large white onion

1 fresh jalapeño, stemmed

2 garlic cloves, unpeeled

2 tablespoons extra-virgin olive oil

Flaky sea salt and freshly ground black pepper

½ cup water

FOR ASSEMBLY

Vegetable oil, for frying

12 mini (5-inch) tortillas (or regular tortillas, to get fewer entomatadas, or cut regular tortillas smaller. Save the scraps for chilaquiles!)

1 10-ounce package Cotija cheese, crumbled

½ white onion, thinly sliced (½ cup), for garnish

Large parsley leaves on stems, fried in oil about 30 seconds until crisp, for garnish (optional)

Preheat the oven to 400°F. Place the tomatoes, onion quarter, jalapeño, and garlic cloves in a baking dish. Drizzle with 1 tablespoon of the olive oil and sprinkle generously with salt and black pepper. Roast until browned and very tender. Transfer to a blender, removing and discarding the garlic peel. Add the water and blend until very smooth.

Heat the remaining tablespoon of olive oil in a medium saucepan and fry the sauce over medium heat until slightly thickened. Season to taste with salt and black pepper.

Meanwhile, add enough vegetable oil to half-fill a small saucepan and heat to 350°F. Fry one tortilla at a time for about 30 seconds, flipping once, until lightly fried but pliable. Using tongs, take the tortilla out while shaking off any excess oil. Then, dip the tortilla into the tomato sauce and turn to coat. Transfer to a board and fill with crumbled Cotija. Roll up like a cigar and transfer to a serving platter. Repeat with the remaining tortillas, tomato sauce, and cheese.

Spoon some additional tomato sauce over the entomatadas. Garnish with thinly sliced white onion and sprinkle with additional cheese and fried parsley (if using) and serve.

Here, I'm teaching you how to make one of the many variations of birria. This one is beef-based and has an assortment of chiles that will serve as its adobo. Basically, it's a shredded, marinated, braised piece of meat that you can use for tacos, served in its broth, or make quesadillas with like we're doing here. What you can't change are the traditional toppings, which are a ton of white onion and cilantro.

My cousin Valeria ate these and told me to retire from everything else and open a place to sell only these tacos. I considered it for a month, but here I am with this book. *Serves 10*

3 tablespoons extra-virgin olive oil

3 pounds bone-in short ribs (or goat meat, if desired)

2 pounds boneless beef shank

5 dried California chiles, stemmed and seeded

5 dried pasilla chiles, stemmed and seeded

5 dried ancho chiles, stemmed and seeded

6 Roma tomatoes, cored

1 small white onion, quartered

4 garlic cloves, peeled

12 black peppercorns

Juice of 1 orange

1 tablespoon achiote paste

Pinch of cumin seeds

Flaky sea salt

QUESATACOS

2 tablespoons extra-virgin olive oil, plus more for drizzling

12 to 16 small corn tortillas, warmed

3 cups shredded Monterey Jack cheese

Pickled Red Onions (recipe follows)

Chopped fresh cilantro, for garnish (optional)

Chopped white onion, for garnish (optional)

Sliced radishes, for garnish (optional)

Dried oregano, for garnish (optional)

Lime wedges

Heat 3 tablespoons of oil in a large, heavy pot. Working in two batches, sear the short ribs and beef shank on all sides, about 5 minutes total. Return all the meat to the pot and add 8 cups of water. The water should cover the meat by at least ½ inch.

Bring to a boil over medium heat, skimming any foam from the surface. Lower the heat to low and simmer, covered, until the meat is almost tender, about 2 hours. Partially uncover and simmer for 1 hour longer, or until the meat falls off the bones.

Transfer the short ribs and beef shank to a cutting board with a slotted spoon and let cool slightly, then shred the meat and discard the bones. Skim the fat off the broth and strain (I like to put a paper towel in the strainer to get a really clear broth).

Discard any debris in the strainer. Reserve 2 cups of the broth to make the sauce. Return the remaining broth and shredded meat to the same pot.

Meanwhile, soak the dried chiles in warm water until soft, about 30 minutes. Drain and transfer to a blender; add the tomatoes, onion, garlic, peppercorns, orange juice, achiote paste, cumin seeds, and 1 tablespoon of salt, and process until smooth. Add the 2 cups of reserved broth and blend. Work in batches as needed.

Recipe continues

Strain the sauce into the pot containing the shredded beef and broth. Simmer for 30 minutes to blend the flavors, not letting it get too thick. Season to taste with salt. Scoop some of the fat or juices from atop the broth into a bowl; we will use this to make quesatacos.

To make the quesatacos, heat 2 tablespoons of the olive oil in a large sauté pan along with a little bit of the reserved fat and/or juices. Working in batches, add the tortillas and cook for 30 seconds. Top half of each tortilla with cheese. Top the cheese with shredded meat and fold over. Cook until the cheese has melted. Transfer to a plate. Top with pickled onions and any desired garnishes, such as chopped cilantro, chopped white onion, sliced radishes, crumbled oregano, and/or a drizzle of olive oil. Serve with lime wedges.

PICKLED RED ONIONS

Pickled red onions will happily live in your fridge for 3 days and will make a great addition to any sandwich or taco. *Makes about 1¼ cups*

1 large red onion, thinly sliced (about 2 cups)

¾ cup distilled white vinegar

¾ cup water

6 tablespoons granulated sugar

½ teaspoon dried oregano, crumbled

½ teaspoon flaky sea salt

Mix together the red onion, white vinegar, water, sugar, oregano, and salt in a large resealable plastic bag; seal and shake, then refrigerate for at least 24 hours.

With tamales, you'll always find recipes such as this that give you very large quantities. There's a reason behind that: You only want to do this once or twice a year. You can make them for a party and everyone can eat them on that day, or because these freeze perfectly, you can make them ahead and eat them throughout the following months.

You can absolutely make the masa for tamales from scratch, but there are some wonderful freshly made masas for tamales at your Mexican market (make sure you don't buy tortilla masa because they are different). My only suggestion would be that, if the masa texture is thick, remember it needs to be spreadable; you can always add a little warm broth or fat in the form of lard or olive oil to soften the masa.

Chicken in salsa verde is the one tamal filling you'll find across Mexico, from top to bottom. ***Makes 3 dozen tamales***

CHICKEN

2 skinless, bone-in chicken breasts

½ medium white onion

4 garlic cloves, peeled

6 cilantro sprigs

2 bay leaves

1 teaspoon flaky sea salt

SALSA VERDE

1 tablespoon extra-virgin olive oil

½ medium white onion, chopped (about ½ cup)

3 garlic cloves, chopped

10 medium tomatillos, husked, rinsed and quartered

2 fresh serrano chiles, stemmed and seeded if desired

½ teaspoon mixed whole peppercorns

½ cup chopped fresh cilantro

Flaky sea salt and freshly ground black pepper

FOR THE FILLING

1 tablespoon extra-virgin olive oil

1 medium white onion, thinly sliced (about 1 cup)

Flaky sea salt and freshly ground black pepper

FOR ASSEMBLY

1 3-pound bag prepared masa (plant-based or traditional)

1 1-pound bag corn husks, soaked in water for 3 hours (weigh them down so they are fully submerged!)

1 1-pound package frozen banana leaves, thawed (to line the steamer; or use corn husks or clean kitchen towels; optional)

Crema Mexicana, for serving (sour cream is fine; I grew up with it)

Recipe continues

To make the chicken, combine the chicken breasts, onion half, garlic cloves, cilantro sprigs, bay leaves, and salt in a medium, heavy saucepan. Add enough water to cover by 2 inches. Bring to a boil over high heat. Lower the heat to medium-low and simmer until the chicken is cooked through. Remove from the heat and let cool slightly. Line a strainer with a paper towel and strain the broth, discarding the vegetables; reserve the broth for the salsa verde. Remove the cooked meat from the bones, shred, and set aside.

To make the salsa verde, heat the olive oil in a large, heavy saucepan over high heat. Add the onion, garlic, tomatillos, serranos, and peppercorns. Sauté until the tomatillos turn olive green. Add 1½ cups of the reserved chicken broth and bring to a boil over high heat. Lower the heat to medium-low and simmer until almost all the liquid evaporates and the vegetables are soft. Remove from the heat, let cool slightly, add the cilantro, then blend. Season to taste with salt and black pepper.

To complete the tamale filling: Heat the tablespoon of olive oil over high heat. Add the onion and sauté until translucent, about 8 minutes. Add the chicken and sauté for 5 minutes to combine the flavors. Add the salsa verde and bring to a boil over high heat. Lower the heat to medium-low and simmer for 10 minutes. Season to taste with salt and black pepper.

To assemble and steam the tamales: Spread a scant ¼ cup of masa on each corn husk, then about 2 tablespoons of the chicken filling. Enclose the filling by folding up the corn husks. You can use corn husks to add a tie to the tamales.

Fill a tamal steamer with water and line with banana leaves, corn husks, or damp, clean kitchen towels. Transfer the tamales to the prepared steamer, standing them upright with their opening facing up. Cover with banana leaves, additional corn husks, or a damp kitchen towel. Steam until cooked through, about 1 hour. Remove from the steamer and let cool slightly.

Serve with crema Mexicana.

DINNERS
en Casa Marcela

Every once in a while, I like to throw my family and students a curveball. I find my students are more willing to experiment with new dishes after our classes, and my goal is to help get you out of the rut of cooking the same old thing. What's different in this dish is the combination of salmon with cheese, which is untraditional. The queso fresco is whipped, which you never see in Mexican cuisine. But I love experiencing that superfamiliar cheese and flavor profile in a new way.

When I cook salmon filets at home, I go for wild-caught sockeye, but for this you need thick, chunky cubes for a kebab that can withstand the heat without drying out. So, look for thick center-cut Alaskan salmon, so you can make 1½-inch cubes. As for the fish sauce, it's supposed to stink! Add a few drops and it will enhance the flavor of your kebabs. *Serves 4*

2 pounds fresh, center-cut salmon pieces, cut into 1½-inch cubes

GLAZE

3 large garlic cloves, very finely minced

1 teaspoon flaky sea salt

8 peppercorns

1 teaspoon chipotle chile (from a can of chiles in adobo; or just the adobo for less heat)

1 teaspoon apple cider vinegar

¼ cup pure maple syrup

1 tablespoon soy sauce

A few drops of fish sauce

Lemon halves

FOR SERVING

Whipped Queso Fresco (recipe follows)

Toasted Hazelnut Arroz Verde (page 109)

Soak bamboo or wooden skewers in water for 30 minutes before starting, if not using metal skewers. Thread 4 or 5 salmon pieces on each skewer. You can add any vegetables here, like asparagus or zucchini, if you have some in the fridge!

For the glaze, you need to mash the garlic, salt, and peppercorns until very fine, either in a molcajete or by bashing with a muddler in a bowl. Stir in the chipotle, vinegar, maple syrup, soy sauce, and fish sauce. Place the kebabs on a rimmed baking sheet and brush with your glaze.

Heat a large cast-iron skillet over high heat. Cook the kebabs until browned on all sides, about 2 minutes per side. While cooking, brush with any remaining glaze. While you are searing the kebabs, sear the lemon halves, cut side down, alongside them in the same pan.

Serve with the whipped queso fresco and toasted hazelnut arroz verde.

SALMON KEBABS with Whipped Queso Fresco

WHIPPED QUESO FRESCO

Familia: Don't be afraid. I know this may be new for you and that you might never have put cheese in a food processor with additional liquid. Trust me here. It's delicious.

To ensure the dish's success, make sure you process the cheese to an incredibly smooth, nongrainy texture. You cannot overwhip the cheese, so be bold! *Makes about 1 cup*

8 ounces queso fresco

¼ cup sour cream

1 tablespoon extra-virgin olive oil

3 tablespoons whole milk

½ teaspoon flaky sea salt

½ teaspoon freshly ground black pepper

⅓ cup minced fresh chives

In a food processor, whip together all the ingredients, except the chives, until very smooth, about 5 minutes—do not underwhip. Transfer to a medium bowl and fold in the chives. Adjust the seasonings. Store in an airtight container in the fridge. It can be made a day ahead.

GAME CHANGER

@christina_g_gonzalez

For the love of all that is good...LET THE RICE REST! And then let it rest some more! Season in layers, dress the greens, save the peeled skins from your chiles and make a salt with them, boil your tomatillos until they're olive green—don't let them get too bitter. Only make enough salsa for one day, preferably one meal. It doesn't keep well. Use the molcajete for anything!

TOASTED HAZELNUT ARROZ VERDE

This one has become a regular here at Casa Marcela. Once you get down the pilaf method of cooking rice, which is basically getting a good, nutty sauté on the rice before adding the liquid, try different combinations. Poblanos and pine nuts would be great. Parsley and almonds. Dill and hazelnuts. Whatever you choose, be patient and really wait for the rice to turn translucent while you're sautéing it. You know it's ready when you can smell it becoming nutty and toasted. That makes all the difference.

The hazelnuts are essential. You need that earthy, crunchy, buttery, fatty counterpoint to all that green freshness that comes from the cilantro and gets absorbed by the rice. *Serves 6*

1 medium white onion, chopped (about 1 cup)

1 medium tomatillo, husked and rinsed

½ bunch cilantro

2 garlic cloves, peeled

1 teaspoon flaky sea salt

2 tablespoons melted unsalted butter

3 cups unsalted chicken broth

RICE

1 tablespoon extra-virgin olive oil

2 cups long-grain white rice (I use basmati)

HAZELNUTS

2 tablespoons unsalted butter

¾ cup chopped hazelnuts

In a blender, combine the onion, tomatillo, cilantro, garlic, salt, melted butter, and broth and blend on high speed until completely smooth.

To cook the rice, heat the oil in a large saucepan over high heat. Add the rice and sauté until nutty, about 3 minutes, stirring continuously. Add the broth mixture and bring to a boil over high heat. Lower the heat to medium-low, cover, and simmer until the rice is tender, about 17 minutes.

In a small skillet, melt the butter over medium-high heat. Add the hazelnuts and stir until toasted, about 3 minutes.

Add to the finished rice and gently stir in. Let the rice rest for 10 to 15 minutes before serving.

HATCH CHILES
Stuffed with Calabacitas

These stuffed chiles are not traditional chiles rellenos. Here, the filling overflows out of the chile and is immediately visible, whereas in a chile relleno (like the one on page 72), the filling is hidden as a surprise.

What this recipe really teaches is the quintessential Mexican side dish of calabacitas (zucchini)—a version of which is found in every Mexican home. If you want to bypass the whole process of charring and cleaning chiles to make this composed dish, that's fine—but you *have* to learn how to make calabacitas.

Here you can go for Hatch, poblano, or Anaheim chiles. When preparing the chiles, the goal is to char them *just* enough that you can peel them, but not so much that they fall apart. Leaving them in a bag to steam continues to cook the flesh, so don't leave them longer than a few minutes. You can char and peel them a day ahead, but they further soften while sitting in their juices, so I line a plate with paper towels and then cover them with plastic wrap. Finally, to remove the seeds, don't pull on the veins of the chiles because you will rip the side wall. Instead, use a small spoon to scrape them out gently.

A couple of ingredient tips: Grate your own cheese. Shredded cheese comes with anticaking ingredients, so it won't stick and form clumps; cheese melts better without them. And, to seed the tomatoes, cut them in half on their equator and gently squeeze out the seeds or use your fingers to scoop them out, then chop.

Makes 6 to 8 chiles

1 tablespoon extra-virgin olive oil

½ large white onion, chopped (about ¾ cup)

3 large garlic cloves, minced

4 medium vine-ripened tomatoes, seeded and chopped

2½ cups chopped zucchini (about 2 medium zucchini)

1 cup fresh corn kernels (from 1 ear)

Flaky sea salt

5 cups packed fresh spinach leaves

2 to 3 cups shredded Monterey Jack cheese, divided

Freshly ground black pepper

6 to 8 fresh Hatch, poblano, or Anaheim chiles, charred, peeled, and slit, seeds carefully removed

Heat the olive oil in a large, heavy sauté pan over medium-high heat. Add the onion and garlic and sauté for 3 minutes. Add the tomatoes and sauté for 3 minutes. Add the zucchini, corn, and a pinch of salt and stir to combine. Place all the spinach atop the mixture, lower the heat to medium-low, cover, and cook until the vegetables are tender. Uncover and stir the spinach into the mixture along with 1 cup of the cheese to melt. Season the mixture to taste with salt and black pepper.

Turn on the broiler to HIGH. Stuff each chile generously with the zucchini mixture and arrange all the stuffed chiles in an ovenproof casserole dish. Cover with 1 to 2 cups of the remaining cheese, because deciding how much cheese you want to add here is totally up to you and your heart's desire. I'd go for 2 cups. Broil until browned in spots (watch so they don't burn!!!) and serve while HOT!

Of all the recipes I created for my online cooking classes, this brings me back to my best memories. When I was growing up in Tijuana, there was a point when my mom became too ill to cook. My father, being the Mexican macho that he was, would go nowhere near the kitchen. So, he found a wonderful man named Pedro who came to cook for us when my mom could not. This is one of my favorite dishes he made. Creamy, rich, with a hint of smoke and totally satisfying. When I got off the school bus and ran into the house, I could recognize the smell of it while on the stairs, before I even made it to the kitchen. What I loved about it was the marriage of my American side, the spaghetti, with my supertraditional, comforting flavors like chipotle.

I thought this was a northern Mexico thing because we are so close to the border; we are more prone to take popular American dishes and "Mexicanize" them. Wrong! You can find versions of this recipe by home cooks all across the country. I don't think I've ever seen it on a restaurant menu, but please let me know if I am mistaken. I want to know who serves this because I'm so willing to pay for it!

As for the chipotles, some brands have less adobo, the vinegary sauce the chiles come in. I think it's the best part and, if you don't like spice, just add all of the adobo for flavor and leave out the actual chiles. *Serves 6*

1 pound dried spaghetti

1½ teaspoons extra-virgin olive oil

2 tablespoons unsalted butter

½ medium white onion, chopped (about ½ cup)

3 large garlic cloves, minced

1 large carrot, peeled and chopped

1 large celery rib, chopped

6 Roma tomatoes, cored and chopped, with seeds

2 bay leaves

2 chipotle chiles (from a can of chipotles in adobo), plus 2 tablespoons adobo (from the can)

¼ cup heavy cream

Flaky sea salt and freshly ground black pepper

Cilantro-Parmesan Croutons (optional; recipe follows) and/or Parmesan cheese

Cook the pasta in a large pot of boiling salted water according to the package instructions. Drain, reserving 2 cups of the pasta cooking liquid.

Heat the oil and butter in a very large, heavy saucepan over medium-high heat. Add the onion and garlic and sauté 5 minutes. Add the carrot and celery and sauté for 2 minutes. Lower the heat to medium, add the tomatoes and bay leaves, and cook, stirring occasionally, until all the vegetables are tender, about 15 minutes. Remove the bay leaves.

Working in batches if needed, transfer the mixture to a blender and add the chipotles, adobo, and cream. Add 1 cup of the reserved pasta water, setting aside the remaining cup of pasta water in case you want to add it to the pasta dish at the end. Blend until a smooth sauce. Season to taste with salt and black pepper.

Using a paper towel, wipe off any bits of veggies that had stayed in the large saucepan. Then, strain the sauce back into its original pan. Bring to a boil over high heat, then lower the heat to medium-low and simmer until thickened, about 15 minutes.

Recipe continues

Add the cooked spaghetti to the saucepan and, using tongs, gently incorporate the pasta and the sauce. This will seem totally weird, like it doesn't fit and if you move it around too much, you'll get sauce all over the place. That's okay. Use tongs to carefully submerge the pasta in the sauce. Transfer to a platter and serve with croutons and/or Parmesan cheese.

I am not ashamed to admit that the best way to reheat this is in a microwave.

CILANTRO-PARMESAN CROUTONS

I was watching the chef Nancy Silverton once and loved her method for making croutons. Instead of cutting the bread into squares, she simply rips crouton-size pieces and puts them on the baking sheet. It gives more crusty bits, she says.

Here, I'm going pretty basic, but you can play with the oil you use. You can use a chile oil, a truffle oil, or the oil from salsa macha—you could even add some of the seeds from the macha. They add a lovely crispy bite to the creamy chipotle pasta. *Makes 2 to 3 cups*

4 cups pieces torn baguette or sourdough (uneven ½-inch pieces)

½ cup extra-virgin olive oil

¼ cup freshly grated Parmesan cheese

1 teaspoon garlic powder

Flaky sea salt and freshly ground black pepper

½ cup chopped fresh cilantro

Preheat the oven to 400°F. Toss the bread pieces, olive oil, Parmesan, garlic powder, and plenty of salt and pepper on a large rimmed baking sheet and bake until golden brown and crisp, about 18 minutes. Toss with the cilantro and serve.

We're half Jewish in this household, so latkes are big for us. They're David's favorite thing in the world. But the reality is, if you were to serve this in Mexico, it would simply be referred to as a very recognizable torta de papa.

This recipe is an adaptation from Leah Koenig's book *Modern Jewish Cooking*, plus the salsa verde, of course. To make it plant-based, the egg was removed and replaced with aquafaba, the liquid in which legumes, such as chickpeas, are cooked. The viscous water in a can of drained chickpeas has similar properties to egg whites and can be whipped. Here, we use the liquid to bind the latkes.

You have options here in terms of how you cook the latkes. We have a pretty "healthy" lifestyle, so fried latkes a couple of times a week are perfectly fine by me. If you want to bake them, I highly suggest you invest in a silicone mat. This recipe makes A LOT of latkes, so I prefer to bake them. But you can certainly fry them instead. Get some vegetable oil (I use avocado oil) up to 350°F and fry about 5 minutes per side until golden, then transfer to paper towels to drain. ***Makes about 3 dozen latkes***

Extra-virgin olive oil, for the pan

2 pounds russet potatoes (about 4 medium potatoes), washed, unpeeled

½ medium yellow onion, peeled

½ cup aquafaba (the liquid from canned chickpeas)

⅓ cup all-purpose flour

1 teaspoon flaky sea salt, plus more for garnish

Salsa Verde (purchased, or recipe follows), brought to a simmer, for serving

Chopped fresh herbs, such as cilantro, parsley, mint, and/or chives, for garnish

Preheat the oven to 375°F. Line a large rimmed baking sheet with a silicone mat and brush liberally with olive oil. Using the large holes on a box grater, grate the potatoes and onion into a colander. Place the colander in the sink and, using all the muscles you didn't use in 2020, push on the mixture to extract as much liquid as possible. Transfer the pressed potatoes and onion to a large bowl and mix in the aquafaba, flour, and salt.

Using a ¼-cup measuring cup, scoop a scant ¼ cup of the potato mixture and place on the prepared baking sheet. Repeat with all of the mixture and space the latkes evenly ½ inch apart.

Drizzle with additional oil. Bake until golden brown on the underside, 20 to 25 minutes. Using a thin spatula (I am obsessed with my fish spatula), carefully turn the latkes over. Continue to bake until brown on the bottom side as well, about 20 minutes longer.

Place a thin layer of salsa verde on a plate. Place the latkes atop the salsa verde. Sprinkle generously with chopped herbs and salt, then serve.

SALSA VERDE

You can certainly purchase salsa verde; there are plenty of
yummy and even organic options on the market and, when
heated and topped with latkes and a bunch of fresh herbs,
there's really no way this won't be delicious. I love Herdez
Salsa Verde and they didn't pay me a penny to say that. Here
is my recipe if you wish to make it from scratch. *Makes about
3 cups*

1 tablespoon extra-virgin olive oil

8 medium tomatillos, husked and
   rinsed

½ medium white onion

2 garlic cloves, peeled

4 whole dried chiles de árbol or
   bird's eye chiles, stemmed

1 cup water

2 tablespoons chopped fresh
   cilantro leaves

Flaky sea salt

In a large sauté pan, heat the oil over medium-high heat.
Add the tomatillos, onion, garlic, and chiles. Cook for about 7
minutes, or until the tomatillo skins are browned.

Transfer the onion, garlic, and chiles de árbol to a blender,
add the water, and blend until smooth. I like to blend the
chiles first to break them down before adding the tomatillos.

Add the sautéed tomatillos and the cilantro and pulse a few
times to break down into a salsa. Season with salt to taste.
Pour the salsa into a serving bowl and serve.

PLANT-BASED LATKES
AND SALSA VERDE

This tastes like a traditional enchilada, but we're not using the traditional enchilada method—we're baking the tortillas instead of frying them. The most important part of either technique is to coat the tortilla with fat, otherwise you get a soggy tortilla once it is filled. The mark of a good enchilada is that it's made with a tortilla that doesn't fall apart or get soggy because of the sauce.

This one does require some solid prep, but you will be able to use these techniques and subrecipes over and over again when modifying other recipes to make them plant-based or slightly healthier.

I don't go crazy over calories or worry about fat too much because that is not my personal issue. We're a small family of small Mexicans. For us, it's more about balance and clean ingredients. Enough indulging so that the kids (and I) don't feel restricted. But here, you could easily add cheese and use crema Mexicana instead of cashew cream. And these would be awesome with shredded chicken.

You also have options with the filling. I used potatoes because I don't love the sweetness of sweet potatoes or butternut squash, but you can cook those exactly as you would the potatoes and it would work.

Note: You *must* soak the cashews ahead of time for the sauce to be creamy.

Serves 2 to 4

ROASTED POTATOES

1 16-ounce can chickpeas, drained (optional)

1¼ pounds Yukon Gold potatoes, peeled and cubed (about 1-inch pieces)

¼ cup chopped fresh parsley

1 teaspoon flaky sea salt

2 tablespoons extra-virgin olive oil

"CREAMY" CHIPOTLE SALSA

2 tablespoons extra-virgin olive oil

1 large white onion, chopped (about 1½ cups)

2 large garlic cloves, sliced

5 medium vine-ripened tomatoes (about 1½ pounds), chopped, with seeds

1 cup plus 2 tablespoons water, divided

2 tablespoons chipotles in adobo from a can (use only the sauce if you don't like heat)

1 bay leaf

⅛ teaspoon dried oregano

⅛ teaspoon ground cumin

¼ cup cashews, soaked in water for 3 hours or overnight

½ teaspoon distilled white vinegar

Flaky sea salt and freshly ground black pepper

FOR ASSEMBLY

8 corn tortillas

Extra-virgin olive oil, for brushing

Shredded lettuce or Iceberg Salad (recipe follows)

Crema Mexicana or any vegan cream, such as cashew cream (optional)

Recipe continues

To roast the potatoes, preheat the oven to 350°F. Toss the chickpeas (if using), potatoes, parsley, salt, and olive oil on a large rimmed baking sheet to combine. Bake until the potatoes are tender, about 1 hour, tossing once or twice during baking. Mash slightly. Season if necessary. Keep warm.

To make the "creamy" chipotle salsa, heat the olive oil in a large, heavy sauté pan over medium-high heat. Add the onion and sauté for 5 minutes. Add the garlic and sauté for 5 minutes. Add the tomatoes and sauté for 10 minutes. Add 1 cup of the water, plus the chipotles, bay leaf, oregano, and cumin, and bring to a boil over high heat. Lower the heat to medium-low and simmer for 15 minutes. Remove the bay leaf and let cool.

Drain the cashews, and combine them in a blender with the vinegar, remaining 2 tablespoons of water, and a pinch of salt. Process until smooth. Add the chipotle mixture and blend until very smooth. Season to taste with salt and black pepper.

Brush the tortillas with olive oil, then place in a single layer on a large rimmed baking sheet and bake at 350°F for 10 minutes. They should be pliable. Place about ½ cup of the salsa in a shallow dish or round cake pan. Dip the tortilla in the salsa, then transfer to a plate and fill with a scant ⅓ cup of the potato filling and roll up like a cigar. Transfer to a serving platter. Repeat with remaining tortillas and filling. Top the enchiladas with some of the remaining salsa. You can freeze any leftover salsa.

Top with shredded lettuce or iceberg salad and crema (if using). Serve hot!

ICEBERG SALAD GARNISH FOR ANY MEXICAN DISH

This is a garnish for any Mexican dish. Dressed lettuce makes *all* of the difference. Iceberg wilts very quickly, so I wait to dress and toss right as I am going to serve. A good trick is to shred it and let it sit in a bowl with ice and water in the fridge while you cook everything else. Just make sure to drain *really* well before using. **Makes about 2 cups**

2 cups shredded iceberg
  lettuce

3 radishes, thinly sliced

Extra-virgin olive oil

Red wine vinegar

Dried oregano

Flaky sea salt and freshly
  ground black pepper

Just before serving, place the lettuce and radishes in a medium bowl. Drizzle with olive oil and add a splash of vinegar. Sprinkle with oregano, salt, and pepper and toss to combine.

This was inspired by a breakfast that I had on the beach in Tulum with my sister. We both love eggs Benedict and finally found a version that combined the traditional procedure of poaching eggs and topping them with a creamy sauce, but with the Mexican flair of serving it on a sope.

The freshest eggs yield the prettiest poached eggs. If they are old, you can strain the raw eggs, one at a time (without breaking the yolk), through a fine-mesh strainer before poaching. The excess thinner whites create more wisps.

If using purchased sopes, make sure they are thawed and heated. Brush them with oil and heat on a large, rimmed baking sheet in a 400°F oven for 15 minutes, or deep-fry them in 375°F oil for 5 minutes. **Serves 6**

½ head purple cabbage, shredded (4 to 5 cups)

¼ cup extra-virgin olive oil

⅓ cup red wine vinegar

Dried oregano

Flaky sea salt and freshly ground black pepper

1 tablespoon distilled white vinegar

6 large eggs

2 cups (or more) refried beans (page 60, or purchased), warmed

6 Sopes (page 59, or purchased), heated

Tomatillo Hollandaise (recipe follows)

Chopped fresh cilantro, for garnish (optional)

Za'atar, for garnish (optional)

First, we will create our cabbage slaw by mixing together the cabbage, olive oil, red wine vinegar, and a heavy seasoning of oregano along with salt and pepper in a large bowl. Set aside.

Bring a medium pot, filled two-thirds full with water, to a boil over high heat. Add the distilled white vinegar. We will do one egg at a time. Crack an egg into a bowl, making sure the yolk doesn't break. Create a vortex by quickly spinning a large spoon in water. Carefully slip the egg into the center of vortex. Cook for 4 minutes. Using a slotted spoon, transfer to a paper towel to drain. Sprinkle with salt and pepper. Cook the remaining eggs, one by one, in the same manner.

Place about ¼ cup of refried beans on each warm sope. Top with a spoonful of cabbage slaw. Top each with one egg. Cover half of the egg with tomatillo hollandaise. Sprinkle it with cilantro and/or your favorite seasoning. Za'atar is great for this!

EGGS BENEDICT...*but Mexican*

TOMATILLO
HOLLANDAISE

This mimics the silky texture of a traditional hollandaise without the risk of the butter and eggs breaking in the sauce. It doubles as a great dressing for potato salad or a cactus paddle salad. Use it anywhere you want a creamy dressing. *Makes about 1½ cups*

4 medium tomatillos, husked and rinsed

⅛ medium white onion (a small wedge)

1 fresh serrano chile, stemmed and seeded (or ½ if you don't want too much heat)

½ medium avocado, pitted and peeled

Leaves from ½ bunch cilantro

2 tablespoons crema Mexicana

1 teaspoon distilled white vinegar

Flaky sea salt and freshly ground black pepper

Bring a medium pot of salted water to a boil over high heat. Add the tomatillos, onion wedge, and serrano and boil for 3 minutes. Turn off the heat and let cool slightly. The tomatillos should be olive green. Transfer the tomatillos, onion, and serrano along with the avocado, cilantro, crema, and vinegar to the blender and blend until smooth. Season to taste with salt and black pepper.

EGGS BENEDICT...BUT MEXICAN

QUINOA CEVICHE TOSTADAS

This salad feels like you're eating a ceviche because of the ingredients you're using—lime, cilantro, onion, tomato, and serrano chiles—but it's fully plant-based, really good for you, and a great weeknight dinner solution. It's simple to put together and incredibly satisfying! You can have it as a tostada or as a salad on its own. Choose to top it with grilled salmon, chicken, or even steak. *Makes 4 to 6 tostadas*

4 to 6 corn tortillas

2 cups water

1 cup uncooked golden quinoa

Flaky sea salt and freshly ground black pepper

¼ cup extra-virgin olive oil, plus more for drizzling

¼ cup freshly squeezed lime juice (from 2 to 3 limes)

1 cup diced tomatoes (about 2 Roma tomatoes)

½ medium white onion, diced (about ½ cup)

1 cup finely chopped fresh cilantro

2 fresh serrano chiles, stemmed, seeded, and finely chopped

Avocado slices, for serving

Fresh cilantro leaves, for serving

Preheat the oven to 400°F. Place the tortillas on a large rimmed baking sheet. Bake until crispy, about 10 minutes. Remove from the oven and set aside.

In a medium saucepan, bring the water and quinoa to a boil over high heat. Lower the heat to low, cover, and simmer until the liquid has been absorbed, 15 to 20 minutes. When the quinoa is done cooking, remove from the heat and set aside to completely cool.

Transfer the quinoa to a medium bowl, then toss with salt and black pepper to taste plus the olive oil and lime juice, until incorporated. Add the tomatoes, onion, cilantro, and serranos and mix again.

Add the quinoa mixture to each tortilla and garnish with avocado, cilantro, and a drizzle of olive oil, and serve!

GAME CHANGER

@_claudia_caceres_

I learned that I can no longer roast a chicken despatarrada! ¡Me enseñó a amarrarle las patas!

ADOBO-RUBBED SPATCHCOCKED CHICKEN
with Za'atar Roasted Potatoes

We're a chicken-eating family over here and I've tried roasting a chicken more ways than I would like to admit! Spatchcocking, or removing the backbone and flattening it out, is one of my favorites. The chicken cooks a little faster so there's less chance that the breast will dry out. It's a great method with or without the adobo. Simply rubbing with butter, salt, and pepper will give you a perfectly roasted chicken.

To season the potatoes, I go for za'atar, a Middle Eastern spice blend that might be new to you but it will be completely familiar when you add it to this dish, because of its citrusy, nutty, earthy notes. If you don't have it or wish to buy it, just use salt and pepper and maybe some chipotle powder, lemon zest, and garlic powder. *Serves 4*

1 5-pound roasting chicken, spatchcocked

¼ cup extra-virgin olive oil, divided

3 dried pasilla chiles, stemmed and seeded

3 dried guajillo chiles, stemmed and seeded

4 garlic cloves, peeled and smashed

½ cup water

2 tablespoons unsalted butter

1 tablespoon flaky sea salt

2 bay leaves

Pinch of dried oregano

1 tablespoon red wine vinegar

3 pounds baby potatoes, halved

1 lemon, halved and thinly sliced into half-moons

1 tablespoon za'atar (or spices of your choosing)

FOR SERVING

Vinegar-Cilantro Salsa (recipe follows)

Corn tortillas

Preheat the oven to 425°F. Place the chicken, cut side down, on a rack in a large roasting pan and set aside.

Heat 2 tablespoons of the olive oil in a medium saucepan over medium-high heat. Add the pasillas, guajillos, and garlic and turn constantly to toast (not burn!) until fragrant, about 6 minutes. Add the water, butter, salt, bay leaves, and oregano and bring to a boil over high heat. Lower the heat to medium-low and simmer for 10 minutes to blend the flavors. Remove from the heat, remove the bay leaves, and let cool slightly, then blend with the vinegar. Rub this mixture all over the chicken, including under the skin (careful not to rip it!).

Scatter the potatoes and lemon slices all around the chicken and drizzle with the remaining 2 tablespoons of olive oil. Sprinkle with za'atar and carefully toss to coat. Sprinkle everything with salt.

Roast until the chicken registers 160°F at the thigh and the potatoes are tender, between 50 and 60 minutes. Then, broil on HIGH for 5 minutes to brown the chicken on top. Remove from the oven and let the chicken rest, uncovered, for 10 minutes before serving with the potatoes, vinegar-cilantro salsa, and tortillas.

VINEGAR-CILANTRO SALSA

I am obsessed with this topping for any protein or taco because of the unexpected kick of the vinegar. Acidity is a flavor catalyst in all tacos, but you usually expect lime. In my house, and from my mom, it was vinegar, and this is a great representation of that. It's become a staple and philodendron Phil's new favorite. ***Makes about ⅔ cup***

1 bunch cilantro, finely chopped

½ medium white onion, minced (about ½ cup)

⅓ cup extra-virgin olive oil

2 tablespoons red wine vinegar

1 fresh serrano chile, stemmed, seeded, minced

Juice of ½ lemon

1 garlic clove, pressed

Flaky sea salt and freshly ground black pepper

Mix together all the ingredients, except the salt and black pepper, in a small bowl. Then, season to taste.

The process is the same as a traditional ensenada fish taco: to batter and deep-fry a white fish filet. But here we're using salmon, and the addition of the salmon chicharrón (the air-fried salmon skin) takes your tacos to restaurant level. Those chicharrones de salmón will become your next favorite thing to cook, that you can prepare anytime you're making salmon and don't want to throw away the skin.

Can you replace salmon with another fish? You totally can! Any firm, white fish filet will work.

Make your salsa and slaw first so the salt draws out moisture and they get a chance to marinate and the flavors combine. You can use any salsa, but you *must* pair this with the crunchy slaw. ***Serves 4***

1 cup all-purpose flour

1 teaspoon baking powder

Flaky sea salt

1 teaspoon za'atar or chipotle powder (optional)

1 cup beer

1 large egg

Vegetable oil, for frying

2 6-ounce pieces fresh salmon (I like wild-caught with no antibiotics or artificial color) with SKIN ON if you want to make chicharrón

FOR SERVING

12 corn tortillas (purchased or homemade)

Cabbage Slaw (recipe follows)

Salsa Bandera (page 217)

Pickled jalapeños

Crema Mexicana

Lime wedges

For the batter, sift the flour and baking powder into a medium bowl. Whisk in a pinch of salt and the za'atar or chipotle powder. Whisk in $1/3$ cup of the beer. Whisk in the egg. Whisk in the remaining $2/3$ cup of beer. Let the batter rest for 10 minutes.

Pour enough vegetable oil into a large sauté pan to come 1 inch up the sides and heat to 350°F. Carefully remove the skin from the salmon. To make salmon chicharrón, place the salmon skin in an air fryer at 350°F and air-fry until crisp but not too dark, 10 to 15 minutes. Cut the salmon into 1-ounce strips. Dip each in the batter and shake to remove any excess batter. Working in batches, place 3 strips in the oil at a time and fry until golden brown, about 2 minutes per side. Transfer to paper towels to drain the excess fat.

To serve, warm your tortillas. Place 1 strip of fish in each. Top with the slaw, salsa bandera, jalapeños, and a drizzle of crema. Garnish with the chicharrón. Serve with lime wedges.

TACOS *de* SALMÓN

CABBAGE SLAW

This is a regular old vinegar-based slaw with habanero that is an essential component of a fried fish taco. I don't like that much heat, so I leave the habanero out. ***Makes about 2 cups***

½ white cabbage, shredded (4 to 5 cups)

6 radishes, halved and thinly sliced

2 shallots, thinly sliced

¼ cup extra-virgin olive oil

¼ cup red wine vinegar

Dried oregano, to taste

½ habanero chile, minced (optional)

Flaky sea salt and freshly ground black pepper, to taste

Mix together all the ingredients in a large bowl. Serve.

Nothing wrong with divorce when it involves two freshly made salsas. If you've never had this before, this will be your new favorite way to have eggs for breakfast. The red salsa is a little spicier, and the salsa verde is a little more mellow with its jalapeño. So, you can choose which side of the plate you want to load with more sauce, or you can gently combine the two. It's important, though, that your yolks are still soft because the magic of huevos divorciados is the new sauce that is created by mixing either salsa with the yolk. *Serves 2 to 4*

SALSA ROJA

4 Roma tomatoes, cored

medium white onion,
   separated into layers

2 fresh serrano chiles

1 garlic clove, peeled

2 tablespoons water

Flaky salt and freshly
   ground black pepper

Extra-virgin olive oil

SALSA VERDE

6 medium tomatillos,
   husked and rinsed

¼ medium white onion,
   separated into layers

1 fresh jalapeño chile

1 garlic clove, peeled

2 tablespoons water

Extra-virgin olive oil

¼ cup chopped fresh
   cilantro (optional)

Flaky sea salt and freshly
   ground black pepper

Extra-virgin olive oil

4 to 8 small corn tortillas
   (5 inches in diameter)

4 to 8 fresh hoja santa
   leaves (optional)

4 to 8 large eggs

Crumbled queso fresco,
   for garnish

Chopped fresh cilantro,
   for garnish

Avocado slices, for serving

To make the salsa roja, place the tomatoes, onion, serranos, and garlic clove in a dry comal or cast-iron skillet and char, turning occasionally, until blackened in spots, about 15 minutes.

To make the salsa verde, in a separate pan (or once you remove salsa roja from the pan you used), char the tomatillos, onion, jalapeño, and garlic clove in a similar manner. Remove the stems from the chiles and, optionally, the seeds.

Transfer the salsa roja mixture to a blender, add the water, blend, and set aside. Rinse the blender, then transfer the salsa verde mixture to the blender, add its water, blend, and set aside.

Heat two medium saucepans over high heat. Add a little olive oil to each. Pour the salsa roja into one saucepan and the salsa verde into the other. Lower the heat under each pan to medium-low and simmer until the sauces thicken slightly, about 8 minutes. Add a little chopped, fresh cilantro to the salsa verde, if you like. Season both salsas to taste with salt and black pepper.

You will cook two huevos divorciados at a time. In a large, heavy saucepan over high heat, heat enough oil to come ¼ inch up the sides of the pan. Add 2 tortillas and push down into the oil. Fry for 1 minute. Carefully place 1 hoja santa leaf (if using) in the center of each tortilla. Carefully crack 1 egg onto each hoja santa leaf (or center of each tortilla). Using a spoon, carefully spoon the hot oil over each egg. Cover and cook just to set eggs, about 2 minutes. Transfer each topped tortilla to paper towels to drain very quickly. Transfer to an oval plate. Top 1 egg with salsa roja and the other with salsa verde. I like to keep the yolk visible. Sprinkle with the queso fresco and cilantro. Serve with avocado slices.

MEX-ITALIAN CHICKEN THIGHS
with Roasted Tomatillos

My kids love this dish because of the crispy chicken skin. You are essentially creating a confit where the chicken cooks in its own fat. The flavor comes from the smoky and tangy dressing, and the roasted tomatillos are the perfect counterpoint for the succulent and juicy chicken. When picking your tomatillos, go for a medium size and look for smooth pieces with no cracks or bruises. The bigger ones are too bitter, and the smaller ones burn quickly. *Serves 4 to 6*

6 bone-in chicken thighs with skin

¾ cup Mex-Italian Dressing (page 48), or purchased Italian dressing

2 pounds medium tomatillos, husks removed, very well rinsed

1 tablespoon extra-virgin olive oil

1 teaspoon any garlicky-citrusy seasoning you like

Flaky sea salt and freshly ground black pepper

Place the chicken thighs in a large resealable plastic bag, add the dressing, and toss to coat. Let stand at room temperature for an hour, moving the thighs occasionally to make sure they are evenly covered in the marinade.

Preheat the oven to 475°F. Toss the tomatillos with the olive oil, seasoning, salt, and pepper and transfer to a large rimmed baking sheet. Roast until browned and caramelized, about 30 minutes.

Heat a large cast-iron skillet over high heat. Remove the thighs from their bag, shaking off as much of the marinade as possible. Add all the thighs to the skillet, skin side down, and cook until browned, about 12 minutes. It's important that the thighs are snug as a bug as they will create steam and moisture and won't brown too much. Transfer the skillet to the oven and continue to cook, skin side down, 7 minutes longer. Remove the skillet from the oven and carefully flip the chicken skin side up. Return the skillet to the oven and continue to cook for 10 minutes, or until fully cooked.

Let stand for 10 minutes before serving. Transfer to a platter, surround with the roasted tomatillos, and serve.

This is simply the best way I've found to make a delicious steak. I'm asking for a bone-in ribeye, but this method works for most steaks. Here, I ask for a 1½-inch-thick steak, so be mindful of that. The thickness of your steak can change your cooking time. Also, the number of steaks you can cook is dependent on the size of your pan. My cast-iron skillet can fit two of these steaks comfortably at the same time. If you want to cook more steaks, I suggest you sear two at a time, transfer them to a large rimmed baking sheet, and then sear a second set for a maximum of four steaks. The time your steak spends in the oven will determine its doneness:

※ For a rare steak (130° to 135°F), you would cook in the oven for about 6 minutes.

※ For medium rare (140°F), you would cook in the oven for about 7 minutes.

※ For medium (150° to 155°F), you would cook in the oven for about 9 minutes.

Makes 2 big steaks

2 tablespoons unsalted butter

2 tablespoons extra-virgin olive oil

4 to 6 garlic cloves, peeled and smashed

3 rosemary sprigs

3 thyme sprigs

2 1¼ - to 1½-pound (each) bone-in ribeye steaks, left at room temperature for 30 minutes before cooking, seasoned with flaky sea salt and freshly ground black pepper

Preheat the oven to 415°F. Melt the butter and oil together in a large, heavy cast-iron skillet over high heat. Add the garlic and herbs and cook, stirring frequently, about 40 seconds. Push the herbs and garlic to the side and add the steaks. If they are too close together, they will not caramelize and it is better to cook them one at a time.

Sear the steaks for 2 minutes per side, placing the garlic and herbs atop the steaks if they begin to get too brown. If you seared the steaks one at a time, now combine both steaks in the same cast-iron pan. Pour any gathered juices over the steaks, and place in the oven.

Roast to your desired doneness, about 7 minutes for medium rare. Let stand for 10 minutes before slicing. Serve with the garlic and herbs.

EL PERFECT RIBEYE

EL PERFECT RIBEYE

FRIED FLOR de CALABAZA QUESADILLAS

This is a traditional Mexican breakfast food. Every hotel across Mexico during brunch will serve this and a huitlacoche quesadilla. You can purchase the flor de calabaza (squash blossoms) at a farmers' market, or if you're lucky, you can find them online in season (usually midsummer). You can choose to just make the quesadillas out of cheese, or you can sauté some shiitake mushrooms with garlic and thyme and use that in place of the flowers.

To get fresh tortilla masa, your best bet may be to call up a local tortilleria and ask if they will sell you 2 pounds of their fresh masa. ***Makes 10 to 12 fried quesadillas***

Avocado or vegetable oil

2 pounds fresh tortilla masa

4 to 6 cups fresh squash blossoms

3 to 4 cups shredded cheese (Monterey Jack or quesadilla)

FOR SERVING

Avocado slices

Hot sauce

Crema Mexicana (optional)

Shredded iceberg lettuce (optional)

In a medium sauté pan with high sides, add enough avocado or vegetable oil to come halfway up the sides. Heat over medium heat to 350°F.

Line the top and bottom halves of a tortilla press with a sheet of plastic wrap or a resealable plastic bag. Using about ¼ cup of tortilla masa, make a thick patty and add to the lined press. Press gently to make a ⅛-inch-thick tortilla. Peel back the top plastic, place some flowers and a little cheese on half of the tortilla, leaving a narrow, bare margin along its curved edge, and then use the bottom part of the plastic to help fold the masa over to form a semicircular quesadilla, pressing lightly around the edges to seal. Repeat to make a few quesadillas at a time.

When ready to fry, remove the quesadillas from the plastic wrap. Carefully slide them into the hot oil and fry until golden, about 5 minutes. Keep warm wrapped in a kitchen towel while you assemble and fry more. These are best served as soon as each batch is ready. Serve with avocado and hot sauce, plus crema Mexicana and shredded iceberg lettuce, if you like.

SEA BASS IN ADOBO TACOS
with Grilled Pineapple–Serrano Salsa

This adobo usually is for chicken, but you can use it on any protein and it will be delicious. In terms of the fish, I use bass here, but you can use a side of salmon or any filet you want; you just have to adjust the cooking times. If it's a 3-pound side of anything, it will be the same cooking time.

As for the adobo, you will only use about half to rub over the fish. It is very difficult to make a smaller amount of it. The best idea for the leftover portion is to put it in a resealable plastic bag and freeze it; it lasts for six months or more.

The banana leaves here do impart some subtle flavor, but their use is more about the presentation of the dish. Go ahead and line your baking sheet with parchment paper instead if you like. ***Serves 8 to 10***

1 tablespoon avocado oil

3 garlic cloves, peeled

1 teaspoon dried oregano

½ teaspoon ground cumin

½ teaspoon freshly ground black pepper

¼ teaspoon ground cloves

4 dried guajillo chiles, stemmed, seeded, and cut into 2-inch chunks

⅓ cup pineapple juice

¼ cup distilled white vinegar

2 tablespoons achiote

Flaky sea salt

2 banana leaves, the length of your baking sheet (optional)

1 3-pound side of skinless sea bass (or any other fish)

FOR SERVING

Warm corn tortillas

Grilled Pineapple–Serrano Salsa (recipe follows)

Lime wedges

To make the adobo, in a small casserole, heat the avocado oil over moderately high heat. Add the garlic and cook, stirring occasionally, until slightly browned, approximately 1 minute. Add the oregano, cumin, black pepper, and ground cloves and cook until fragrant. Add the guajillos and cook until blisters form, about 30 seconds. Add the pineapple juice, vinegar, and achiote and bring to a boil over high heat. Remove from the heat and let stand for 5 minutes. Then, transfer the mixture to a blender and puree until smooth. Season with salt to taste.

Place the banana leaves on a large rimmed baking sheet to form a long X, or line the baking sheet with parchment paper. Place the fish on the prepared pan. Spread about half of the adobo over the top of the fish. Cover and transfer to the fridge for 1 hour.

Preheat the oven to 350°F. Remove the fish from the fridge, uncover, and bake until just cooked through, about 35 minutes.

Serve the adobo fish with warm tortillas, pineapple serrano salsa, and lime wedges, to assemble into tacos.

GRILLED PINEAPPLE–SERRANO SALSA

As fantastic as fish or meat seasoned with adobo are on their own, you really need this bright, fresh pineapple and the crispy, citrusy heat from the serrano to complete the taco. The new sauce that is created from the juices of the pineapple salsa and the adobo is what makes the dish. *Makes 4 cups*

2 tablespoons extra-virgin olive oil, plus more for brushing

½ medium pineapple, peeled and sliced into ¼-inch-thick rounds (about 5 slices)

1 fresh serrano chile, stemmed

½ medium red onion, sliced into half-moons (about ½ cup)

1 bunch cilantro, minced

2 tablespoons distilled white vinegar

Flaky sea salt and freshly ground black pepper

Preheat a grill pan over high heat. Brush with a little of the oil. Add the pineapple and serrano. Cook the pineapple until you see black grill marks, about 5 minutes per side. Remove and set the pineapple aside to cool. Continue to cook the serrano, if necessary, turning every couple of minutes, until blackened in spots. Remove the serrano and let cool. Add the red onion and cook until also blackened in spots, about 3 minutes per side. Transfer the onion to a medium bowl.

Chop the serrano and pineapple (removing the center core). Transfer to the bowl that contains the red onion. Add the cilantro, the 2 tablespoons of olive oil, and the vinegar and gently toss to coat. Season to taste with salt and black pepper.

SEA BASS IN ADOBO TACOS WITH GRILLED
PINEAPPLE–SERRANO SALSA

If you grew up eating tuna fish sandwiches with jalapeños like I did, this is the elevated version. All the familiar flavors, just a new presentation. I published a very similar recipe fifteen years ago in my first book, but then I happened to find gorgeous grilled artichoke hearts at the market, and I added them just to the top of the pickled vegetables and it was magic. You can leave them out, or use jarred artichoke hearts packed in oil.

For safety, before adding the water and vinegar to the hot oil, sprinkle just a few drops of the liquid into the oil. If the oil splatters, then it needs to cool before adding the full recipe amount. Continue to test the oil with more sprinkles of vinegar and water until no splattering occurs. Then it is safe to add the full amount of vinegar and water. *Serves 4 to 6*

Tía Laura's TUNA-STUFFED ANAHEIM CHILES

8 fresh Anaheim chiles

2 6-ounce cans albacore tuna in water, drained

1 cup fresh peas (from 1 pound in the shell), or canned, or frozen and thawed

½ cup fresh corn kernels (from 1 ear), or canned, or frozen and thawed

3 tablespoons mayonnaise

Flaky sea salt and freshly ground black pepper

¾ cup sliced carrots

⅔ cup extra-virgin olive oil

2 garlic cloves, peeled

2 small red onions, halved and thinly sliced (about 1½ cups)

⅔ cup distilled white vinegar

2 teaspoons crumbled dried oregano

2 bay leaves

5 or 6 oil-packed grilled artichoke hearts, for garnish (optional)

Over a gas flame, char the Anaheims on all sides until blackened. Alternatively, you can do this in a dry cast-iron skillet; it'll just take a little longer. Place them into a resealable plastic bag to sweat for about 10 minutes. Remove the chiles from the bag and, using paper towels, wipe off the charred skin. With a paring knife, slice the chiles down the center to just reveal the inside, being careful not to fully cut them in half. With a spoon, scoop out the seeds and the vein, keeping the stem and the rest of each chile intact. Place the chiles in a 9-by-13-inch glass baking dish and set aside for stuffing.

Combine the tuna, peas, corn, and mayonnaise in a small bowl. Season with salt and black pepper and set aside.

Cook the carrots in boiling salted water over high heat until just crisp-tender, about 3 minutes. Drain and set aside to cool. Heat the olive oil in a large saucepan over medium heat. When the oil is hot, add the garlic and red onions and cook until the onions are slightly cooked, but still crispy, 5 minutes. Add ⅔ cup of water and the vinegar and bring to a simmer. Add the carrots, oregano, and bay leaves. Simmer until the vegetables are crisp-tender and almost all of the liquid has evaporated, 8 minutes. Let cool slightly.

Stuff the peppers with the tuna mixture. Place back in the baking dish; they should fit snugly. Pour the warm pickled mixture over the stuffed chiles and allow to cool to room temperature. Cover and chill for 2 hours or overnight. Serve cold, topped with the artichoke hearts, if desired.

GUAJILLO STEAK *and* POTATOES

This dish is a guisado, a sautéed saucy meat dish with vegetables. While most folks eat their guisados in a taco, my mom used to give us crusty baguette slices or even toasted white bread because it better absorbs the tomato sauce. Either way, it's a very comforting dish that is both easy to put together and impressive to present on the table! *Serves 6*

3 tablespoons extra-virgin olive oil

6 Roma tomatoes, cored

6 medium tomatillos, husked and rinsed

3 garlic cloves, peeled and smashed

2 dried guajillo chiles, stemmed, seeded, and torn into pieces

½ cup water

2 pounds thinly sliced petite sirloin (sold for milanesa-style dishes), seasoned well with flaky sea salt and freshly ground black pepper or any seasoning of your choice

2 large russet potatoes, peeled, halved lengthwise, and cut into ¼-inch half-moons

½ medium white onion, thinly sliced (about ½ cup)

Flaky sea salt and freshly ground black pepper

FOR SERVING

Crusty French bread or tortillas

Avocado slices (optional)

Pickled jalapeño chiles

Chopped fresh parsley

Heat 2 tablespoons of the olive oil in a large, heavy saucepan over medium-high heat. Add the tomatoes, tomatillos, garlic, and guajillos. Bring to a boil over high heat. Cover, lower the heat to medium-low and simmer until everything softens, about 10 minutes. Transfer to a blender, add the water, and blend into a sauce.

Heat the remaining tablespoon of olive oil in a large, heavy saucepan. Add the meat and sauté for 8 minutes over medium heat. Cover and cook for 25 minutes to release the juices and until the meat is tender. Add the potatoes and cook for 5 minutes. Add the onion and cook for 5 minutes, stirring frequently.

Strain the sauce into the pan and bring to a boil over high heat. Lower the heat to medium-low, cover, and simmer for 20 minutes. Season to taste with salt and freshly ground black pepper. Serve with crusty French bread or warm tortillas for tacos, with avocado if desired. Garnish with the pickled jalapeños and parsley.

Just darn good chicken. A straightforward recipe that solves the weeknight dinner dilemma. The magic here is in the salsa; fresh arugula makes all the difference. I have massive amounts growing in the garden and it goes in my soups, my sandwiches, my pasta, and now even in my salsa. It's just so peppery and good. *Serves 4*

POLLO CON PAPAS

3 pounds baby potatoes, halved

Extra-virgin olive oil for drizzling

Your favorite seasoning that includes onion and garlic powder/flakes

1 5-pound chicken, spatchcocked (split in half by removing backbone and flattening)

2 tablespoons unsalted butter, sliced into pats

Flaky sea salt and freshly ground black pepper (optional)

1 lime, thinly sliced into rounds

1 head garlic, halved on its equator

ARUGULA SALSA VERDE

2 medium tomatillos, husked and rinsed

1 fresh jalapeño chile, stemmed and seeded

4 green onions

1 bunch arugula

½ bunch cilantro

2 tablespoons extra-virgin olive oil

1 tablespoon red wine vinegar

Juice of ½ lemon

For the pollo con papas, preheat the oven to 400°F. Place the potatoes in a baking dish large enough to hold the chicken. Drizzle lightly with olive oil. Sprinkle with your favorite seasoning. Place the spatchcocked chicken, cut side down, on the potatoes. Place pats of butter under the skin of chicken, all over. Drizzle with about 1 tablespoon of olive oil. Add more seasoning (or just salt and black pepper) and scatter the lime slices all over. Place the halved garlic in the pan, buried in the potatoes.

Roast, basting the chicken with pan juices at least three times while cooking, until the internal temperature of the chicken reaches 165°F at the thigh, about 50 minutes. If the chicken is not cooked through but beginning to brown, loosely cover the breast with a piece of foil.

Combine all the salsa ingredients in a blender and blend until smooth. Season to taste with salt and black pepper. Serve with the roasted chicken.

POLLO CON PAPAS
with Arugula Salsa Verde

HAM AND GRUYÈRE CREPES
with Poblano Sauce

Once you learn how to make these crepes, the possibilities are endless. You do have to stick to a savory profile, but you can stuff them with cream cheese and smoked salmon. Or swap out the poblano for half a can of chipotles and have a chipotle cream sauce. Sautéed spinach and/or mushrooms with some thyme and garlic—or any veggie sauté, really—would make a great filling.

You can also play with adding flavor to the crepe batter. I added a tablespoon of dried flaked chipotles and they added so much flavor, but you can also use any chopped fresh herbs. If you could get your hands on epazote and add a couple of teaspoons of it, freshly chopped, it would be divine! Play with them! Let me know what you come up with! *Makes 10 to 12 crepes*

CREPE BATTER

¾ cup whole milk

2 large eggs

1 large egg yolk

½ cup all-purpose flour

4 tablespoons (½ stick) unsalted butter, melted

1½ teaspoons flaky sea salt

POBLANO SAUCE

2 tablespoons extra-virgin olive oil

1 tablespoon unsalted butter

½ medium white onion, chopped (about ½ cup)

2 garlic cloves, minced

3 fresh poblano chiles, charred, peeled, seeded, and diced

¾ cup crema Mexicana

¼ cup water

Flaky sea salt and freshly ground black pepper

FOR COOKING AND ASSEMBLING CREPES

Unsalted butter

10 to 12 small ham slices

2½ cups grated Gruyère cheese (or any melting cheese)

½ bunch cilantro, chopped

½ cup crema Mexicana

½ white onion, thinly sliced

To make the crepe batter, combine the milk, eggs, egg yolk, flour, butter, and salt in a blender and blend on high speed for about 3 minutes. Let sit for 20 to 30 minutes before making the crepes.

To make the poblano sauce, in a medium skillet, combine the oil, butter, onion, garlic, and poblanos and sauté for 5 minutes over medium heat. Then, add your crema and water and bring to a boil over high heat. Lower the heat to medium-low and simmer for 3 minutes. Remove from the heat and let cool slightly. Transfer to a clean blender and blend on high speed until very smooth. Season to taste with salt and black pepper.

To cook the crepes, butter an 8-inch nonstick skillet or crepe pan and heat over medium heat. Pour in about $^1/_3$ cup of batter and gently swirl to coat the bottom of the pan. Crepes are like kids; you always screw up the first one. Cook for about 2 minutes. Using a rubber spatula, carefully go around the edge of the crepe to unstick it from the pan and flip it over. Cook for 2 more minutes. I'm cool with a little color on the crepes. Stack on a plate when done.

To assemble, place your ham in a separate medium skillet over medium heat and cover with the cheese; once melted, place some ham and cheese on each crepe, then fold each crepe in half, then in half again to form a rounded triangle, and top with the poblano sauce. You can also serve rolled crepes by topping each with ham and cheese and rolling up like a cigar. Garnish with cilantro, crema Mexicana, and white onion.

CHICKEN MILANESAS
with Creamy Morita Noodles

I developed this recipe to top the Creamy Morita Noodles, but chicken milanesas can certainly exist on their own. I grew up with milanesas topped with tomato sauce and cheese, or in a torta, or even to stuff a poblano. Or just on their own with a sprinkle of lime juice and some fresh salsa on the side. ***Makes 8 milanesas***

½ cup extra-virgin olive oil, divided

2 10-ounce (each) boneless, skinless chicken breasts

⅓ cup all-purpose flour

2 teaspoons garlic salt

2 large eggs

1 cup panko bread crumbs

½ cup finely shredded Parmesan cheese

2 teaspoons dried oregano

1 teaspoon garlic flakes

1 teaspoon onion flakes

1½ teaspoons fresh thyme

1½ teaspoons fresh rosemary, chopped

Flaky sea salt and freshly ground black pepper

Creamy Morita Noodles (recipe follows), for serving

Preheat the oven to 375°F and oil a large rimmed baking sheet with olive oil.

Split each chicken breast in half, then butterfly cut each portion to make four pieces. Place the chicken pieces on a cutting board, cover with plastic wrap, and pound them to an even ¼-inch thickness with the flat side of a meat mallet or a rolling pin.

In a shallow dish, whisk together the flour and garlic salt. In a second shallow dish, whisk the eggs together until blended. In a third shallow dish, toss together the panko bread crumbs, Parmesan cheese, oregano, garlic flakes, onion flakes, thyme, and rosemary. Season the chicken pieces with salt and pepper on each side. Coat the chicken breasts, one at a time, on both sides, in this order: First, dredge a breast in your flour mixture, then transfer to the whisked egg, coat well, lift, and let any excess run off. Now, transfer to the panko mixture, coating both sides while pressing the mixture onto the chicken to fully cover.

Place the breaded chicken, in a single layer, on the oiled baking sheet (or two sheets to be able to space the chicken apart). Lightly drizzle the breaded chicken breasts with olive oil. This will ensure that they don't dry out during baking. Transfer to the oven and bake until golden brown and cooked through, about 1 hour, checking occasionally.

Serve over the noodles.

CREAMY MORITA NOODLES

These are so decadent. There's something magical that happens when you take a traditional Italian cream sauce base and just add some Mexican dried chiles, like moritas. You're not getting a ton of heat, just smoky deliciousness. *Serves 8 to 10*

12 to 15 ounces dried egg noodles

2 tablespoons unsalted butter

1 tablespoon extra-virgin olive oil

½ medium white onion, minced (about ½ cup)

4 garlic cloves, thinly sliced

1 to 2 tablespoons morita chile flakes

6 Roma tomatoes, chopped, with seeds

1 cup heavy cream

1 cup grated Parmesan cheese

1 bunch basil, chopped

Flaky sea salt and freshly ground black pepper

1 tablespoon fresh oregano, chopped (optional)

In a large pot of salted water, boil the noodles according to the package instructions. Drain, reserving 1 cup of the pasta water.

Heat the butter and oil in a wok or large sauté pan over high heat. Add the onion and garlic and cook for 3 minutes. Add the chile flakes and cook for about 30 seconds. Add the tomatoes and simmer for about 4 minutes. Add the reserved pasta water and cream, then simmer for about 10 minutes to reduce the sauce. Stir in the Parmesan and basil. Season with salt and black pepper to taste, and with the oregano (if using). Add the noodles, stir, and serve.

GAME CHANGER

@kerrieneu

This seems so basic and easy but it was big for me. When we were cooking the Chicken Milanesas, I learned not to cover the cookie sheet with anything if you want that crispy finish. I cover my cookie sheet all the time for easy cleanup—hence my soft bottom chicken! You have to let the chicken touch the cookie sheet and get hot and crispy. This time my chicken turned out amazing!

CHICKEN MILANESAS
WITH CREAMY MORITA NOODLES

SOUPS
Caldos

The goal of this soup is to make you feel like you're biting into a buttered, slathered corn on the cob. The flavors are really simple because the corn is the star, and for that reason, the corn you choose is really important. My preference is sweet white corn, but any corn on the cob will work. I just don't want you to use frozen, thawed corn for this—it's just a different animal entirely.

Two things to know: The first is that smooth soups are a sign of a good cook, so if you're out there telling people I taught you this, you better blend this to silky perfection or strain it free of clumps. The other is that once you understand how a roux works, you can use it for any other soups or sauces. A roux is simply a mixture of equal parts butter and flour that are whisked, over heat, in your pan. You then whisk in your soup or your sauce (or your gravy!) and you get a beautiful sheen and body as a result. *Serves 4 to 6*

4 tablespoons (½ stick) unsalted butter, divided

⅓ medium white onion, finely chopped (about ⅓ cup)

2 garlic cloves, minced

2½ cups fresh corn kernels (from about 2 large ears of corn)

2 cups chicken broth

1 tablespoon all-purpose flour

1 cup heavy cream, mixed with 1 cup water

Flaky sea salt and freshly ground black pepper

FOR ASSEMBLY

4 to 6 sourdough small round loaves, top sliced off and insides removed and reserved for the croutons

1 fresh poblano chile, charred, peeled, seeded, deveined, and finely chopped

Crema Mexicana

Extra-virgin olive oil

Basil Poblano Parmesan Croutons (recipe follows)

Melt 3 tablespoons of the butter in a medium saucepan over medium heat, add the onion and garlic, and sauté until translucent, about 4 minutes. Then, add your corn and sauté for 5 to 8 minutes.

Add the chicken broth, bring to a simmer, and transfer to a blender. Let cool briefly, then blend until very smooth.

To make the roux, in a large saucepan, combine the remaining tablespoon of butter and the flour. Mix to make a paste. Slowly pour in your watered-down heavy cream while whisking to get rid of any unwanted clumps, then bring to a boil over high heat and turn off the heat.

Transfer the corn mixture to your roux mixture and whisk until incorporated. Season to taste with salt and black pepper. Pour the soup into the hollowed-out sourdough loaves and top with the garnishes and croutons.

BASIL POBLANO PARMESAN CROUTONS

The reason that these croutons soak up so much of the flavor of this pesto is that the pieces of bread are torn. Those ragged edges absorb all of the pesto, and then become crunchy when they dry out. They're amazing. *Makes 4 to 5 cups*

¾ cup extra-virgin olive oil

½ large bunch basil

1 poblano chile, seeded and chopped

2 garlic cloves, peeled

½ cup grated Parmesan cheese

Bite-size pieces of sourdough, torn from bread bowls

Flaky sea salt and freshly ground black pepper

Preheat the oven to 350°F. In a blender, combine your olive oil, basil, poblano, garlic, and Parmesan cheese. Blend until the flavors are fully combined. In a large bowl, toss the bread pieces with your pesto, plus salt and black pepper to taste. Transfer to a large rimmed baking sheet and bake for 30 to 40 minutes, or until crisp.

Lulu, a wonderful woman who has been a part of my family for over a decade, talked me through this recipe, which is basically meat, slow-cooked until very tender, that is seasoned with a red chile sauce with floating fresh masa dumplings. A dish that warms both body and soul.

These dumplings are much more forgiving than tortillas, especially since we will be adding fat to them. It's *really* important that if you purchase the masa (which I suggest), make sure it's not tamal masa! If you cannot find fresh masa, you can make it yourself according to the masa harina package instructions.

You can break this recipe into two parts. Part one is cooking the beef, which you can do a day ahead. Part two is letting it cool down and refrigerating it, then bringing it to a boil the next day before continuing. *Serves 10*

BEEF

3 pounds boneless beef chuck pot roast

10 cups water

½ medium white onion

1 medium carrot

1 large celery rib

2 bay leaves

1 tablespoon flaky sea salt

FINISHING THE TESMOLE

3 tablespoons extra-virgin olive oil

4 large garlic cloves, peeled and smashed with the side of a knife

4 dried morita chiles (these are HOT; sub with 2 guajillos if you want less heat), stemmed and ripped into pieces

3 dried guajillo chiles, stemmed and ripped into pieces

1 dried ancho chile, stemmed and ripped into pieces

½ hoja santa leaf (optional; if you can't find, simply omit)

2 cups vegetable broth

1 tablespoon distilled white vinegar

1 teaspoon flaky sea salt

2 chayote squash, peeled, quartered, and cored

1 fresh ear of corn, cut into 10 pieces

10 baby red potatoes

Flaky sea salt and freshly ground black pepper

Fresh cilantro or parsley, for serving

CHOCHOYOTES

1½ pounds fresh tortilla masa

¼ cup chopped fresh herbs (mint, hoja santa, epazote; a mix of all three; or just mint)

2 teaspoons lard or duck fat

Pinch of flaky sea salt

To make the beef, place all the beef ingredients in a very large pot and bring to a boil over high heat, about 30 minutes. Lower the heat to medium-low, cover, and simmer for 1 hour. Uncover and skim all the brown foam from the top. Remove and discard the vegetables and bay leaves so you only have broth and beef in the pot. You can do this a day ahead. Let cool completely, cover, and refrigerate.

Recipe continues

Finish the tesmole: Bring the beef and broth to a boil over high heat, Meanwhile, in a separate large, heavy sauté pan, heat the oil over high heat. Add the garlic and cook for 1 minute. Add all the dried chiles and the hoja santa (if using) and stir frequently for 2 minutes. Add the vegetable broth, vinegar, and salt. Cook for 6 minutes to soften the chiles. Remove the chile mixture from the heat and let cool slightly. Blend until smooth, then add to the beef mixture. Add the chayotes, corn, and potatoes, cover, lower the heat to medium-low and simmer for 1 hour. Season to taste with salt and black pepper.

To make the chochoyotes (masa balls), simply knead the masa, herbs, lard, and a pinch of salt until well combined. Take a heaping tablespoon of the mixture and roll into a ball. Flatten into a thick disk and, using your thumb, make an indentation in the center. Add to the pot of soup and simmer for 10 minutes.

Serve garnished with fresh cilantro or parsley.

There's nothing particularly innovative about this soup, but it's perfect for a weeknight meal. If you really want to take it to the next level, go to the trouble of making the mushroom and jalapeño chicharrones.

You can make this soup using poblano, Hatch, or Anaheim chiles! Also, if you want to keep it vegan, you can use cashew cream (thinned out). I don't recommend almond milk or coconut milk because of flavor and consistency, but you can certainly give it a shot! *Serves 4*

2 tablespoons extra-virgin olive oil

1 medium white onion, chopped (about 1 cup)

4 garlic cloves, minced

2 large fresh poblano chiles, stemmed, seeded, and chopped

4 cups chopped zucchini (from 2 or 3 zucchini)

4 tablespoons (½ stick) unsalted butter, diced

1 thyme sprig, or 1 teaspoon fresh thyme leaves

Pinch of dried oregano

4 cups vegetable broth

½ to 1 cup heavy cream or crema Mexicana

Squash blossoms and unsalted butter, for garnish (optional)

Chicharrón de Chile (page 211, optional)

Heat the oil in a large, heavy pot over medium heat. Add the onion, garlic, and poblanos and stir continuously to soften, about 8 minutes. You're doing what is called sweating an onion. You don't want it to caramelize or turn brown; you just want it to soften.

Add the zucchini, butter, thyme, and oregano and continue to stir to soften, 20 to 25 minutes. Add the broth, increase the heat to high, and bring to a boil. Lower the heat to medium-low and simmer to blend the flavors, about 10 minutes.

Remove from the heat and let cool slightly, then stir in the cream and process the mixture in a blender in two batches. Return the soup to the pot and bring to a boil over high heat, then lower the heat to medium-low and simmer to thicken, 10 to 15 minutes. Season to taste with salt and black pepper. Serve with squash blossoms and butter, and/or chicharrón de chile, if desired.

POBLANO *and* CALABACITA CREAM SOUP

CALDO TLALPEÑO

This is like tortilla soup, but with garbanzo beans and chipotle. You could certainly cook the garbanzo beans yourself or even in the chicken broth but, for ease, we are using canned. Make sure you rinse them well.

Use a fine-mesh strainer to strain your broth and if you want it *really* clear, line the strainer with paper towels to catch any debris. *Serves 6 to 8*

CHICKEN

1 whole chicken breast (2 halves attached with bone, about 3½ pounds)

1 head garlic, halved on its equator

½ medium white onion

3 bay leaves

1 teaspoon assorted peppercorns (I use red, black, and one Malaysian long peppercorn)

16 to 20 cups water

1½ tablespoons flaky sea salt

2 large carrots, peeled and cut into rounds

1 15-ounce can garbanzo beans, drained and rinsed (add 2 cans if you really like them)

TOMATO PUREE

2 tablespoons extra-virgin olive oil

1 medium white onion, chopped (about 1 cup)

3 large garlic cloves, peeled and smashed

6 Roma tomatoes, chopped, with seeds

1 dried guajillo chile, stemmed and seeded

1 7-ounce can chipotles in adobo (I like Embasa brand)

Flaky sea salt and freshly ground black pepper

GARNISHES

2 medium avocados, pitted, peeled, and diced

6 corn tortillas, cut into thin strips (I like to cut each tortilla into 4 thick strips and then crosswise into very thin strips, so it looks like a nest) and fried until crisp

Oaxaca or panela cheese in strings or cubes (I add like ¼ cup to every serving, so plenty!)

Lime wedges

Fresh cilantro leaves

To cook the chicken, place it in a large pot with the halved garlic head, onion half, bay leaves, peppercorns, and enough water to fill the pot. Add the salt, cover, and bring to a boil over high heat. Lower the heat to medium-low, leave covered, and simmer until the chicken is fully cooked, about 50 minutes. Drain the chicken and RESERVE the broth, discarding the vegetables. Shred the chicken when cool enough to handle, discarding the chicken bone. Return just the broth to the clean pot and keep covered over low heat. Do not add the carrots or garbanzos yet.

To make the tomato puree, heat the oil in a large, heavy sauté pan over medium-high heat. Add the chopped onion and smashed garlic and sauté for 6 minutes. Add the tomatoes and guajillo and sauté until the tomatoes have released juices, about 10 minutes. I like to take the back of my wooden spoon and mash the tomatoes to release all their juices and break them apart. Add all the adobo sauce from the canned chipotles and anywhere from 1 to 4 chiles, depending on how much heat you want. I usually add two. Sauté for 2 minutes longer. Season to taste with salt and black pepper.

Transfer the tomato mixture to a blender and blend on high speed until very smooth. To the chicken broth, add the carrots, garbanzos, and tomato puree and bring to a boil over high heat. Lower the heat to medium-low and simmer for 10 minutes to cook the carrots. Season well to taste with salt and black pepper.

To serve, place a handful of shredded chicken in a shallow bowl and top with the soup. Add the avocado, tortilla strips, and any of the other garnishes. I like to add a whole chipotle from the can to add even more heat!

GAME CHANGER

@christihanks

I learned that the toppings take the soup to the next level—something acidic (lime), something creamy (avocado), something crunchy, some spice, some fresh herbs :-)

For this soup, you have to soak the beans the night before. I like to use a brand called Rancho Gordo cassoulet white beans, but you can use any bean you want. Your cooking time will vary depending on the bean. Just look for them to be really tender so they puree nicely. Adding cream is optional and will add silkiness to the soup. I like to serve this soup in small bowls, so everyone gets a good soup-to-garnish ratio. I need tortilla strips in every bite. It's also a very filling soup, so you don't want to serve it in a very large dish. *Serves 4 to 6*

1 cup dried beans, soaked overnight in plenty of water (you can't overdo it)

½ medium white onion, unsliced, plus 1 medium white onion, thinly sliced (about 1 cup)

1 large celery rib

2 bay leaves

1 medium carrot, halved

10 peppercorns (optional)

2 tablespoons extra-virgin olive oil

2 garlic cloves, minced

Crema Mexicana (optional)

Flaky sea salt

4 corn tortillas, halved and cut into very thin strips

4 tablespoons (½ stick) unsalted butter

¼ cup vegetable oil

Queso fresco, for garnish

⅓ cup chopped fresh cilantro, for garnish

1 medium avocado, pitted, peeled, and diced, for garnish

Chile oil, for garnish (optional)

Put the beans and their soaking liquid in a large, heavy pot. Add plenty of water to cover the beans by at least 3 to 4 inches. Add the onion half, celery, bay leaves, and carrot. You could add peppercorns here, if you like. Bring to a rolling boil over high heat and let boil for 10 minutes. Lower the heat to medium-low and simmer gently until the beans are tender, about 1 hour. Drain the beans, discarding the vegetables and peppercorns but reserving the liquid; you should have about 6 cups of it.

Heat the olive oil in a large, heavy pot over medium heat. Add the sliced onion and garlic and sauté until translucent but not browned, about 10 minutes. Add the beans and sauté for 5 minutes. Stir in 4 to 5 cups of the bean cooking liquid (discard the rest). Bring to a boil over high heat, lower the heat to medium-low, and simmer to blend the flavors, about 10 minutes. Remove from the heat, let cool slightly, then transfer to a blender and blend, working in batches if needed. You could add ¼ cup of crema Mexicana to the blender, but it is not necessary. Season to taste with salt.

To fry the tortillas, heat the butter and vegetable oil in a large sauté pan to 350°F. Fry the tortilla strips until crisp. Transfer to paper towels to drain. Sprinkle with salt while warm.

Transfer the soup to small bowls. Top each with plenty of tortillas, queso fresco, cilantro, avocado, chile oil, if using, and crema Mexicana.

CREMA *de* FRIJOL

SOPA de ALBÓNDIGAS

These albóndigas are so easy and so yum. Not much to tell you here except all you need is some lime wedges and a really good hot sauce. There's always the option of stirring in some adobo from some canned chipotles but my little ones aren't into that much heat, so I usually skip it. Maybe just put the can of chipotles in adobo on the table...*in a nice little serving bowl, familia* (not in the can!). **Serves 6**

1 tablespoon vegetable oil

½ small white onion, chopped (about ⅓ cup)

⅓ cup uncooked long-grain rice

2 tablespoons chopped fresh cilantro

2 tablespoons chopped fresh mint

1 pound ground sirloin beef (or half sirloin and half ground lamb)

Flaky sea salt and freshly ground black pepper

1 medium carrot, cut into rounds

1 whole fresh serrano chile

1 Yukon Gold potato, skin on, diced

2 tablespoons tomato paste

8 cups vegetable broth

2 zucchini, diced (about 2½ cups)

In a large, heavy pot, heat the vegetable oil over medium-high heat. Add the onion and cook until translucent, about 5 minutes. Remove from the heat and let cool slightly.

In a medium bowl, combine the cooked onion, rice, cilantro, mint, ground meat, 1 teaspoon of salt, and 1 teaspoon of black pepper. Using wet hands, shape the meat mixture into 20 to 22 1-inch-diameter meatballs and set aside.

Combine the carrot, serrano, potato, tomato paste, and vegetable broth in a large saucepan and bring to a boil over high heat. Add the meatballs and zucchini, lower the heat to low, and simmer until the meatballs are cooked through, about 20 minutes. Season the soup with salt and black pepper to taste.

Chile, cheese, and potato soup is a traditional and very comforting soup combo that so many of us grew up with. The panela cheese doesn't fully melt; it retains its shape but becomes soft and warm, and the floating chiles and papas are very best friends when they all make it into the same bite. I added a little Casa Marcela flair with the en croûte part. Keeps it all safe and warm! Make sure your bowls are ovenproof! *Serves 4 to 6*

2 tablespoons extra-virgin olive oil

½ large white onion, chopped (about ¾ cup)

2 garlic cloves, minced

6 Roma tomatoes, chopped, with seeds

1 teaspoon dried oregano

6 cups chicken or vegetable broth (if purchased, low-sodium), warm or at room temperature

4 cups chopped skin-on white potatoes

4 cilantro sprigs

2 bay leaves

1 teaspoon mixed peppercorns

4 Anaheim chiles, charred, peeled, and chopped into 1-inch pieces

2 cups cubed panela cheese

Flour for dusting a rolling pin (or wine bottle)

1 1-pound package frozen puff pastry, thawed in fridge overnight

1 large egg beaten with 1 tablespoon of water, for egg wash, or ½ cup almond milk

Chopped fresh parsley, for garnish

Salsa macha, for garnish

Preheat the oven to 350°F. Heat the oil in a large, heavy saucepan over high heat. Add the onion and sauté until beginning to brown, about 6 minutes. Stir in the garlic and cook for 4 minutes. Add the tomatoes and cook, stirring occasionally, until very soft, about 10 minutes. Stir in the oregano. Stir in the broth. Add the potatoes, cilantro sprigs, bay leaves, and peppercorns and bring to a boil over high heat. Lower the heat to medium-low, cover, and simmer until the potatoes are tender, about 18 minutes. Once the vegetables are cooked, stir in the Anaheim pieces and cubed cheese.

Meanwhile, using a floured rolling pin, roll out the puff pastry to a ¼-inch thickness. From each sheet (the package should contain 2 sheets) cut 4 squares, each about 7 by 7 inches, adjusting the size of the squares depending on the bowls being used; the pastry should completely cover the top with a ¼-inch overhang. Set the squares aside (don't stack, as they will stick, or use flour-sprinkled parchment paper between them if stacking).

Scoop 1½ to 2 cups of soup into an individual ovenproof bowl. Brush the edge of the bowl lightly with egg wash or almond milk. Carefully place the pastry over the bowl. Press the edges onto the bowl and cut around to create an even ½ inch of overhang. Crimp the edge, if desired. Brush the top with egg wash or almond milk. Working quickly, repeat with the remaining soup and pastry.

Bake until the puff pastry is golden, about 20 minutes. Serve with parsley and salsa macha.

ANAHEIM CHILE, CHEESE, and POTATO SOUP en Croûte

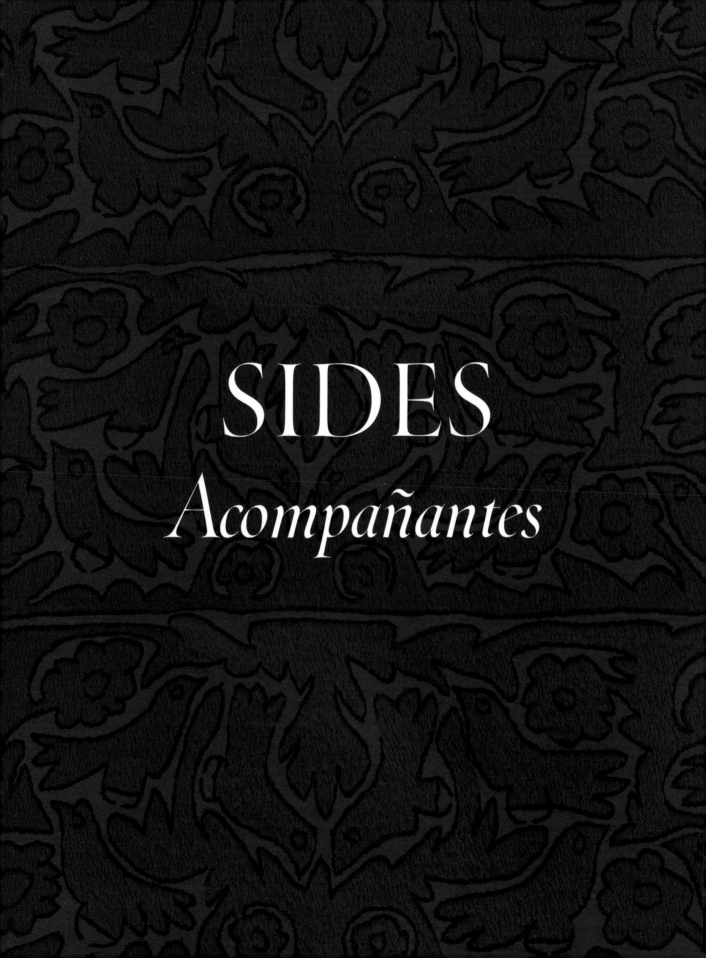

SIDES

Acompañantes

This simple rice dish gets some extra love with spinach and a cheese gratin.

Serves 4 to 6

2 tablespoons unsalted
   butter

⅓ medium white onion,
   chopped (⅓ cup)

1 teaspoon flaky sea salt

1 teaspoon freshly ground
   black pepper

2 cups warm water

1 cup uncooked long-grain
   white rice

1 cup packed chopped
   fresh spinach

1 cup shredded cheese,
   Monterey Jack
   preferred

Preheat the oven to 425°F. Melt the butter in a medium, heavy saucepan over medium heat. Add the onion, salt, and pepper and sauté until golden, about 4 minutes. Add the water, rice, and spinach, mix well, and bring to a boil over high heat. Once boiling, immediately lower the heat to low, cover, and simmer for 18 minutes.

Once the rice is done, remove from the heat, fluff with a fork, and let rest for 15 minutes. Transfer to an oven-safe serving platter and top with the shredded cheese. Place in the oven and bake for 5 to 8 minutes, or until the cheese is golden.

ARROZ *con* ESPINACAS

FIDEO SECO *en* MOLE

Officially my partner Philip's new favorite recipe! Fideo seco is simply very thin, short pasta noodles cooked in the same way as you would cook Arroz Rojo (Mexican rice, page 186): with a flavorful liquid that gets fully absorbed during cooking, hence the name "seco," meaning "dry." The more traditional way is to use a tomato broth, possibly seasoned with chipotle, but adding mole simply makes it the perfect mix of comfort food with added flavor and magic. You can use capellini or angel hair pasta, but you must break it into small pieces with your hands.

Notes on the tomato sauce and mole paste: For the tomato sauce, I took half of a 28-ounce can of San Marzano tomatoes and pureed them with a teaspoon each of onion powder and garlic powder. You can make your own by quickly boiling and peeling six tomatoes with the same seasonings. As for the mole paste, you can use store-bought for this recipe—I have used these brands: Mole Doña María, Juquilita Mole Coloradito, and the Northgate González Market; alternatively, you can use my recipe on page 84. *Serves 6*

2 tablespoons extra-virgin olive oil

1½ cups tomato sauce (see headnote)

8 ounces mole paste (see headnote)

About 3 cups chicken or vegetable broth, divided

Flaky sea salt

14 ounces dried fideo pasta (I use two 7-ounce bags)

2 garlic cloves, peeled and smashed

Crema Mexicana, for garnish

1 medium avocado, pitted, peeled, and sliced

Sesame seeds, for garnish

Chopped fresh cilantro, for garnish

Heat the oil in a large, heavy saucepan over high heat. Add the tomato sauce and bring to a boil over high heat. Lower the heat to medium-low and simmer for 10 minutes. Whisk in the mole paste. Whisk in enough of the broth (about 1½ cups) to get you to 4 cups of the sauce. Season to taste with salt, remove from the heat, and set aside. Keep warm.

Heat a large, heavy sauté pan (that will fit both the fideo and the 4 cups of sauce!) over medium heat. Add the fideo and garlic and stir constantly until golden brown. This is done with NO oil! You have to constantly move the fideo, while adjusting the heat, so that it toasts evenly. When it is a light brown color, stir in the mole sauce. Bring to a boil over high heat, lower the heat to medium-low, cover, and simmer for 10 minutes.

Uncover and stir in 1 cup of the broth (or more if dry). Cover and cook for 5 minutes longer. Adjust the seasoning. Transfer to a platter and serve with crema, avocado, sesame seeds, and cilantro.

CORN-STUDDED FLUFFY WHITE RICE

Delicious, straightforward, and a classic. Can't go wrong with this one! You could add some smoky flavor by adding charred, peeled, and diced chiles like poblanos or Anaheim at the same time as the corn. See photo with the Mex-Italian Chicken Thighs (page 136). *Serves 4 to 6*

2 cups uncooked long-grain white rice (I use basmati)

3 cups water

3 tablespoons extra-virgin olive oil

¾ cup fresh corn kernels, cut from the cob

1 teaspoon flaky sea salt

Combine the rice and water in a medium, heavy saucepan with a tight-fitting lid. Drizzle with the olive oil. Add the corn kernels and sprinkle with the salt. Bring to a boil over high heat without stirring, with the lid ON. When the mixture comes to a boil, remove the lid, stir a couple of times, return the lid, lower the heat to medium-low, and simmer until the rice is cooked through, about 17 minutes. Turn off the heat. Let stand, covered and undisturbed, for 10 minutes. Fluff with a fork, cover for another 10 minutes, then serve.

To make these beans, you need cooked frijoles de la olla (cooked beans in broth) from the recipe that follows. When measuring, just scoop the measuring cup in the pot to collect beans and broth at the same time; don't drain.

You can substitute rinsed canned beans, but will need to add a little broth or water to be able to blend them before frying. Also, you won't have all the additional flavor that comes from the bacon/bones or vegetables you used to cook the beans. You could add some organic vegetable or chicken bouillon (about a tablespoon) to the canned beans to add more flavor. Nothing compares to home-cooked beans, but sometimes you just have to reach for the can…

Compared to Frijoles Machacados (page 60), which are light and basic and can be the base of numerous other dishes, these are packed with flavor and fire and can be eaten on their own as a side. *Serves 4 to 6*

4 cups cooked beans, pinto preferred, with a little of their broth, from Frijoles de la Olla con Tocino (recipe follows), or canned and rinsed

½ cup avocado oil (or lard if you want!)

3 dried chiles de árbol

½ medium white onion, thinly sliced (about ½ cup)

3 garlic cloves, peeled and smashed

Flaky sea salt

In a blender, puree the beans with their broth until smooth. Set aside.

Heat the oil in a large, heavy saucepan over medium-high heat. Add the chiles de árbol, onion, and garlic. Quickly fry the chiles, stirring, for 3 minutes, then remove and reserve. Continue to cook the onion and garlic until golden, about 4 minutes longer. Using a slotted spoon, transfer the onion and garlic to paper towels to drain. Lower the heat to medium-low and CAREFULLY whisk the pureed beans into the oil. Whisk until well incorporated and cook for 5 minutes longer; cook a little more to reduce if you want a thicker consistency. Season to taste with salt and garnish with the reserved fried chiles and the onions and garlic.

FRIJOLES REFRITOS

FRIJOLES DE LA OLLA CON TOCINO

These are similar to the frijoles de la olla used for the Frijoles Machacados (page 60) for sopes, but have the addition of pork in the form of bacon and an optional ham hock.

The beans for this recipe need to be soaked one night in advance and the beans can take two hours to cook! If you are cooking a dish with them on Saturday morning, soak them Thursday night and cook them Friday, so you are not stressed on Saturday morning!

These beans in a bowl with a little cooking liquid, olive oil, a splash of vinegar, salt, and a little cilantro are a great snack—or just eat them with a drizzle of crema. ***Makes 1 large pot of beans***

3 cups dried pinto beans, soaked in water to cover by 3 inches the night before cooking them

½ pound sliced bacon

½ medium white onion

1 medium carrot

1 large celery rib

3 bay leaves

1 ham hock or bone, or marrow bones (optional)

Flaky sea salt

Throw everything into a large pot, including the soaking liquid for the beans, but without adding any salt, and cover with 2 to 3 inches of water. Bring to a rolling boil over high heat. Boil for 10 minutes. Lower the heat to medium-low and simmer, partially covered, until the beans are tender, about 1 hour, adding more hot liquid if the beans are exposed. Season to taste with salt. Remove and discard everything but the beans.

ARROZ ROJO

This is my most popular recipe ever. It's elusive: Many of us grew up with arroz rojo but we didn't get the recipe. We just ate it at home with our moms, so we missed the exact amounts and the exact procedure. As simple as the dish may seem, this is one of the rare occasions where I ask you to stick specifically to times and measurements, so that you can get that perfect Mexicano arroz rojo that you used to have as a kid in Mexico. See photo on page 87.

Serves 6

> There are a few REALLY important tips to ensure you get good, fluffy rice:
>
> 1. Properly sauté your rice before adding liquid to it. It should turn golden and fragrant. Creating that oil/fat barrier will protect the rice from sticking too much.
> 2. Add hot broth, not cold, to the rice.
> 3. Do not uncover the rice while cooking, unless mentioned in the recipe.
> 4. Work quickly when the recipe mentions to add vegetables and to gently stir rice. You want as little steam to escape as possible.
> 5. Letting the rice rest after cooking is the most important step. In fact, rice will have a better texture after completely cooled and reheated the next day.

- 3 cups low-sodium chicken broth
- 1 tablespoon flaky sea salt
- 2 tablespoons extra-virgin olive oil
- 2 cups uncooked white basmati rice
- 1 cup minced white onion (from about 1 medium onion)
- 2 large garlic cloves, minced
- 1 cup canned or homemade tomato sauce
- ½ fresh jalapeño chile, seeded
- ½ teaspoon garlic powder
- 1 cup frozen peas and carrots, thawed

Combine the chicken broth and the salt in a small saucepan and bring to a simmer over medium-low heat. You don't want to reduce it! You just want it to be hot when you add it to your rice.

Heat the oil in a medium, heavy saucepan with a lid over high heat. When very hot, add the rice and sauté, stirring frequently, for about 3 minutes. Add the onion and garlic and stir for 1 to 2 minutes, or until the rice is starting to turn golden and fragrant. Add the tomato sauce and stir to absorb and release any extra moisture, 1 to 2 minutes. Add the hot broth and bring to a boil over high heat. Stir the rice and add the jalapeño and garlic powder. Cover, lower the heat to medium-low, and simmer for 12 minutes.

Quickly uncover and add the peas and carrots to the rice (let them sit at the center for now). Cover and cook for 3 more minutes. Uncover and gently stir the rice to incorporate the tomato sauce (it floats to the top!) and vegetables. Cover and cook for 2 more minutes.

Turn off the heat and the let rice stand, covered, for at least 20 minutes, then season to taste before serving.

GAME CHANGER
@anggar69

The arroz rojo was the one thing I vowed never to cook again because I could not make it. It was undercooked or overcooked. I made it and was taken back to me in Monterrey, Mexico, at the age of 8 and my padrino's mother made this huge pot of arroz rojo with peas and carrots for me. It tasted just like hers and it was the best rice ever!! This rice literally brought me to tears.

GAME CHANGER
@veromend46

Chef, you taught me to use WARM water/chicken stock when making rice so it doesn't stick to the pan. Best simplest thing that has been a game changer for me. So simple but so effective! Gracias!

These potatoes with chorizo are a quintessential Mexican breakfast side that are just as easy as they are delicious. You can make it plant-based by getting soy chorizo and using cashew crema instead of crema Mexicana.

In terms of the chorizo, they all come with a different fat content. The basic method is to just put the link of raw chorizo (without casing!) in a large pan over high heat and use the back of a wooden spoon to break it up. I ask you to sauté until "almost fully cooked" because after its time in the pan, it still gets roasted in the oven with all the other goodies. You can use hot Italian sausage if you don't have chorizo.

Serves 4 to 6

- 6 cups chopped Yukon Gold potatoes (1-inch cubes), unpeeled
- 2 bunches green onion, white and pale green parts only
- 8 ounces chorizo, crumbled and sautéed until almost fully cooked, then transferred to paper towels to drain, cooking fat reserved
- Extra-virgin olive oil, if needed
- ¼ chopped fresh parsley, plus more for garnish
- 1 tablespoon chopped fresh rosemary
- 2 teaspoons chopped fresh thyme
- Flaky sea salt and freshly ground black pepper
- Lime wedges, for garnish

CHIPOTLE CREMA

- 1 to 2 tablespoons chipotles in adobo
- ½ cup crema Mexicana or cashew crema
- 2 tablespoons chopped fresh cilantro
- Juice of 1 lime
- Flaky sea salt and freshly ground black pepper

Preheat the oven to 350°F. On a large rimmed baking sheet, toss the potatoes, green onions, chorizo crumbles, and 3 tablespoons of the chorizo fat (completing with olive oil if you don't have enough chorizo fat), plus the parsley, rosemary, and thyme. Toss to coat. Sprinkle with salt and black pepper. Roast the potatoes in the oven until fully cooked and crisp, golden on the outside, tossing once or twice while roasting, about 50 minutes.

To make the chipotle crema, mix together the chipotles, crema, cilantro, and lime juice in a medium bowl. Season to taste with salt and black pepper.

Serve the potatoes, garnished with additional fresh parsley, with lime wedges and the chipotle crema.

PAPAS *con* CHORIZO, GREEN ONIONS, *and* Chipotle Crema

BRUSSELS SPROUTS *with Guajillos and Piloncillo~Caramelized Pancetta*

Incredibly simple and delicious. One thing, though: When you cook the pancetta in the piloncillo, you end up with delicious, caramelized pancetta bits that happen to be very sticky. Give yourself a nice hand wash and mix that salad the way it's supposed to be mixed, with your hands! Use your fingers to break up the pancetta pieces and scatter them evenly throughout the dish. No need to shred the Brussels sprouts yourself; just purchase the bag of them already thinly sliced.

This is one of those sides that could take probably a few extra ingredients from your pantry, like pepitas or mandarin wedges or chopped dates or any grilled vegetable, really. Sneak in whatever you want that isn't too salty or too briny. You already have bacon, and you want to let the sweetness shine! **Serves 4**

1½ pounds shredded Brussels sprouts (I purchased preshredded)

⅓ cup extra-virgin olive oil, plus more for marble surface (if using)

3 dried guajillo chiles, stemmed, seeded, and cut into thin strips or rings

2 large garlic cloves, minced

Flaky sea salt and freshly ground black pepper

¼ cup grated piloncillo

8 ounces pancetta, cut into small cubes

1 teaspoon chopped fresh thyme

Preheat the oven to 415°F. Toss the Brussels sprouts, olive oil, guajillo strips, garlic, and plenty of salt and pepper on a large rimmed baking sheet. Roast until the Brussels sprouts are browned, about 30 minutes, stirring at about halfway through that time. Meanwhile, place the piloncillo and pancetta in a medium, heavy saucepan over medium-high heat. Cook, stirring frequently, until the pancetta is fully cooked, 4 to 5 minutes. Turn out the mixture onto a silicone mat or oiled marble surface. When just cool enough to handle (be careful: this is molten sugar), break up with your hands and stir in the thyme. Set aside.

Place the roasted Brussels sprouts in a large bowl. Add the cooked pancetta mixture and toss to combine. Add more salt, plus black pepper, if needed. Serve warm or room temperature.

This is an everyday rice to serve with any of the traditional dishes in this book. The technique of adding the lemon zest while you're sautéing the rice is a great way to add another layer of flavor early in the recipe, so it gets really incorporated into the rice.

Serves 4 to 6

3 tablespoons extra-virgin olive oil

½ medium white onion, minced (about ½ cup)

3 large garlic cloves, minced

2 cups uncooked basmati rice

1 tablespoon fresh lemon zest (from 2 lemons)

2¾ cups low-sodium chicken or vegetable broth, warmed

¼ cup fresh lemon juice

¾ cup chopped fresh parsley, divided

1 teaspoon flaky sea salt

¼ teaspoon dried crumbled oregano

2 tablespoons unsalted butter

Heat the oil in a medium, heavy saucepan over medium-high heat. Add the onion and garlic and sauté for 5 minutes without browning. Add the rice and lemon zest and sauté for 2 to 3 minutes. Add the warm broth, lemon juice, $^{1}/_{4}$ cup of the parsley, salt, oregano, and butter and bring to a boil over high heat. Lower the heat to medium-low, cover, and simmer for 19 minutes. Remove from the heat and let stand, covered, for 10 minutes. Fluff with a fork and let stand, covered, for 10 to 15 minutes longer before serving. Garnish with the remaining parsley.

LEMON-PARSLEY RICE

This is another instance where we're using jamaica (hibiscus) for something other than agua fresca, its traditional use. The wild rice, caramelized shallots, Brussels sprouts, and mushrooms combination is a classic on the US side of the border. But the addition of jamaica brings a tart flavor and chewy texture that's unexpected but somehow works. *Serves 4 to 6*

1 cup uncooked wild rice

2 cups uncooked long-grain white rice (I use basmati)

3¾ cups water for cooking white rice

½ cup hibiscus flowers

1 tablespoon unsalted butter, olive oil, or ghee

Flaky sea salt

1 pound Brussels sprouts, quartered

3 cups sliced shiitake mushrooms

4 shallots, thinly sliced

2 garlic cloves, minced

1 tablespoon chopped fresh thyme

½ cup grated piloncillo

3 tablespoons extra-virgin olive oil

Freshly ground black pepper

½ cup chopped fresh parsley

Cook the wild rice in 6 cups of boiling, salted water over medium-high heat for 40 minutes, then drain and keep warm or at room temperature.

Preheat the oven to 350°F. Place the white rice, water, hibiscus flowers, butter, and 1 teaspoon of salt in a medium, heavy saucepan. Bring to a boil over high heat. Lower the heat to medium-low, cover, and simmer until the rice is tender and the liquid is absorbed, about 20 minutes.

Meanwhile, toss together the Brussels sprouts, mushrooms, shallots, garlic, thyme, piloncillo, and olive oil on a large rimmed baking sheet and scatter evenly into a single layer. Sprinkle heavily with salt and pepper. Roast until golden brown, tossing half-way through baking, about 35 minutes.

In a very large bowl, toss together the wild rice, hibiscus-rice mixture, and roasted vegetables. Add almost all of the parsley and toss to combine. Season to taste with salt and pepper. Transfer to a platter and top with the remaining parsley.

JAMAICA WILD RICE *with Caramelized Shallots, Brussels Sprouts, and Wild Mushrooms*

Superdecadent CREAMY POTATO CAKE

What's better than potatoes, cream, and cheese? Tell me. TELL ME! Seriously, this is so easy and so good. It's literally just layers of cream, potatoes, cheese, herbs, and flavor that is really impossible to mess up. Whether you cut this perfectly or make it messy, it's going to end up tasting great.

You could make your life even easier by using a mandoline, but I just cut the potatoes by hand. Also, try to save some of those jalapeño slices so you can use them to top the last layer of cheese for a nice garnish. Don't forget to place the springform pan on a rimmed baking sheet in case some of the cream leaks.

I can eat a third of this by myself, so please be warned and exercise some control. Or don't. *Serves 4 to 6*

Oil or cooking spray, for the pan

1½ cups heavy cream

3 rosemary sprigs

2 pounds yellow potatoes, thinly sliced (can be done with mandoline)

1 very large fresh jalapeño chile, thinly sliced

2 tablespoons extra-virgin olive oil

Flaky sea salt and freshly ground black pepper

2 cups shredded Monterey Jack cheese (or any white melting cheese)

¼ cup freshly grated Parmesan cheese

Preheat the oven to 400°F. Oil or spray a 9-inch springform pan (if you don't have one, use a 9-inch round cake pan), then line with parchment paper cut to fit. Place the pan on a rimmed baking sheet. Do this in case there are any leaks; the baking sheet will catch them, and your oven won't smoke.

Bring the cream and rosemary sprigs to a simmer in a small saucepan over medium heat. Turn off the heat and let stand until cool. Remove the rosemary and save to use as a garnish.

Toss the potatoes, jalapeño slices, olive oil, and a heavy pinch of salt and pepper in a medium bowl. In the prepared springform pan, you will create three layers. For the first layer, scatter one-third of the potatoes over the bottom of the dish, then sprinkle evenly with one-third of the Monterey Jack, then top with one-third of the rosemary-infused cream. Repeat two more times to create the remaining two layers. Top the third layer with Parmesan cheese and the reserved rosemary sprigs.

Cover tightly with aluminum foil and bake for 30 minutes. Uncover and bake for another 30 minutes, then broil until browned in spots. Remove from the oven, let cool for 10 minutes, and remove the springform collar. Cut into wedges and serve.

If this comes out supersoft and tender, it's not a mistake—that's what it's supposed to be. This is not a crumbly American cornbread recipe. It's kind of sticky and supersweet.

It's important that you beat the egg whites properly to stiff peaks, which means that if you turn the bowl over your head, they stay in the bowl and you don't get egg whites all over yourself. That's how you know they're ready. The whites help give the torta de elote its slightly bouncy texture. ***Makes one 8-inch square baking pan***

Unsalted butter and all-purpose flour, for baking dish

Kernels cut from 6 ears white sweet corn

¼ cup sweetened condensed milk

½ pound (2 sticks) unsalted butter, at room temperature

¾ cup granulated sugar

5 large eggs, separated, at room temperature

¾ cup all-purpose flour

1 tablespoon baking powder

1 teaspoon flaky sea salt

Preheat the oven to 350°F and butter and flour an 8-inch square baking pan.

In a blender, process the corn and sweetened condensed milk together until blended but still slightly coarse. Beat the butter and sugar in the bowl of an electric mixer until creamy and smooth, then beat in the egg yolks, one at a time. Sift the flour, baking powder, and salt into a small bowl. Add half of the corn mixture to the butter mixture and mix, then add half of the flour mixture and mix. Repeat with the remaining corn and flour mixtures until just incorporated.

Using very clean beaters, beat the egg whites to stiff peaks in a large bowl. Gently fold the egg whites into the batter. Transfer the batter to the prepared baking pan. Bake until a tester inserted into the center comes out clean, about 1 hour 10 minutes.

Remove from the oven. Let cool slightly then invert onto a platter or serve directly from the pan.

TORTA de ELOTE

CORN TORTILLAS

I think it's disingenuous when a recipe offers an exact ratio of masa to water to make a tortilla. Masa harina varies too tremendously in both texture and moisture content to be able to offer a precise ratio that will work no matter where you are. So, instead of specific quantities of ingredients (basically, you're using just masa harina and water), I offer you the technique and the advice to follow the instructions on the package of masa harina that you purchase. **Makes as many as you want**

Here are the most important tips:

1. When making the masa, err on the side of adding too much water. Dry masa will crack. Steam escapes through cracks and you get no puff. You are looking for a Play-Doh consistency.

2. Always add warm water. It will absorb better and quicker into the masa harina.

3. *Knead* for at least 5 minutes; 10 is best. This is tiring. You'll live. You are pushing water into the masa, which will make it smooth.

4. *Rest* the masa, covered with plastic wrap, for at least 30 minutes. Again, you are letting the water be properly absorbed into the masa.

5. You are looking for an ⅛-inch thickness in your press. Too thick or too thin and puffing is more difficult. I like to line my press with resealable plastic bags because they are *thick*, and it makes it easier to peel off the tortilla.

6. Use a nonstick pan if you are a beginner. I'm not and it's still what I use the most. You can buy an inexpensive nonstick pan at any retailer and it'll work. What won't work is an old pan with the nonstick peeled off. The newer, the better.

7. This is the most important part: *Medium heat;* 30 seconds on side one, 1 minute 30 seconds on side two. Flip a second time and it should puff.

8. They might seem dry and a little hard. You need a cloth or tortilla warmer lined with a clean cloth or anything that will trap the heat. Once they are stacked in there, the residual heat will steam them and make them pliable for tacos.

9. Godspeed…

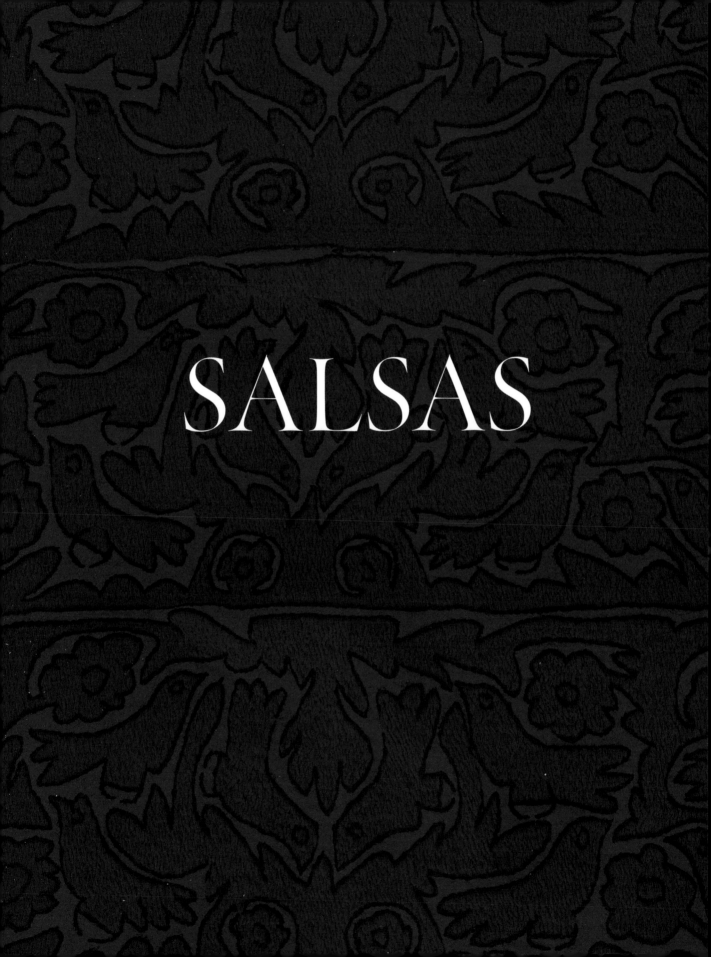

SALSAS

CHIMICHURRI SALSA VERDE

This is much like a chimichurri, but with a little more heat, that you can use to top pretty much any protein, like salmon or any grilled poultry or meat. Because this salsa is not pulverized in a molcajete or blender, make sure you finely mince all the ingredients. Don't be afraid of the whole lemon—it adds a great balance and a more satisfying body and texture to the salsa. ***Makes about 1 cup***

1 bunch cilantro, minced

½ cup peanuts, minced

1 fresh jalapeño chile, seeded, stemmed, and minced

1 fresh serrano chile, seeded, stemmed, and minced

⅓ cup toasted sesame seeds

1 lemon, minced, with peel (yup! the whole thing)

⅓ to ½ cup extra-virgin olive oil

⅓ cup champagne vinegar

1 teaspoon dried oregano

Red pepper flakes, flaky sea salt, and freshly ground black pepper to taste

Mix together all the ingredients and serve.

This salsa is hot from the chile de árbol. If you're new to salsas and spice, this salsa might not be for you…yet. You'll get there! Even though I give you a range of using from five to fifteen chiles, even five is still pretty hot. I developed this recipe for Sopes (page 59), but it can be a table salsa like any other. *Serves 6*

6 medium tomatillos, husked and rinsed

4 Roma tomatoes, cored

4 large garlic cloves, peeled and smashed

5 to 15 dried chiles de árbol (your choice how many to use), stemmed

¼ medium white onion

1 tablespoon extra-virgin olive oil

Flaky sea salt, to taste

Bring a medium saucepan (make sure it's big enough for all the ingredients) of salted water to a boil over high heat. Add everything, except the olive oil and salt, and bring to a boil again. Lower the heat to medium-low heat, cover, and simmer for 10 to 15 minutes, or until all the tomatoes are cooked. Using a slotted spoon, transfer the solid ingredients to a blender (discard any liquid from the pan). Add the oil and blend until smooth. Season the salsa to taste with salt and serve.

BOILED CHILE *de* ÁRBOL SALSA

This is a great example of how beautifully Asian and Mexican flavors work together. You can see this combination all over Baja Mediterranean cuisine. This is a great pairing with the Bacalao a la Vizcaina (page 81). *Makes about 2 cups*

8 fresh güero chiles

1 bunch green onions, white and pale green parts only

¼ cup plus 1 tablespoon extra-virgin olive oil, divided

⅓ cup freshly squeezed lime juice

⅓ cup chopped fresh cilantro

¼ cup soy sauce

1 fresh serrano chile, sliced into thin rounds

½ to 1 teaspoon red pepper flakes

Toss the güero chiles and green onions with 1 tablespoon of the olive oil in a medium bowl. Place the güeros and green onions in an air fryer and air-fry at 350°F until blistered all over and blackened in spots. Alternatively, you can fry them in 350°F oil or broil them; just watch that they don't burn. Place in a shallow dish and add the remaining ¼ cup of olive oil plus all the other ingredients, except the red pepper flakes, and stir to combine. Sprinkle with red pepper flakes at the end. These chiles get better in the fridge after a couple of days.

Homemade HOT SAUCE

Why make your own hot sauce when so many brands are readily available? For one, it just tastes better. For another, it give you a great sense of accomplishment and satisfaction to make your own damn hot sauce. And it also makes an amazing hostess gift, when you put it in a cute glass bottle.

I have added the weight of the chiles (instead of the volume) because I want you to look at the label of the bag at the grocery store. It's hard to get a cup size on dried chiles, so weight is the most accurate way to measure. I must say it doesn't need to be perfect. If it's a 100-gram bag of guajillos, just eyeball half of it.

I love this hot sauce served warm and freshly made. The intensity changes when it cools down, but it is just as delicious. You will be making a whole lot of hot sauce, so have some recycled and clean glass jars ready so you can walk some over to the neighbors. This hot sauce lasts for months in your fridge.

It will take you a minute to stem those chiles (use gloves if you're sensitive to chiles). If you don't use gloves, just don't touch your face (or your privates! LOL) afterward.

Before you email me: There are no substitutions to get you to this exact same sauce. My suggestion is to use whatever you have available and just eyeball about 115 grams total of dried chiles. *Makes a LOT of hot sauce, between 6 and 7 cups*

50 grams dried chiles de árbol, stemmed

50 grams dried guajillo chiles, stemmed

10 fresh chiles piquín (small little balls)

5 whole dried puya chiles

6 cups water

1 tablespoon flaky sea salt

1 tablespoon garlic powder

1 teaspoon dried oregano

¼ teaspoon ground cloves

2 cups apple cider vinegar

1 tablespoon cornstarch mixed with 2 table-spoons water, to make a slurry

Place all the dried chiles and the water in a pot and bring to a boil over high heat. Boil for 5 minutes. Using a slotted spoon, transfer the chiles to the blender. Add 2 cups of the chile cooking liquid and remaining ingredients, except the cornstarch slurry, to the chiles. Blend on high speed until very smooth. Strain the sauce back into the pot. Bring to a boil over high heat and stir in the cornstarch slurry, whisking vigorously for 1 minute.

CHILE OIL CRUNCH

We make this every week at my house. Philip is obsessed. I have to stop myself from topping every single soup, Mexican dish, or pasta with this condiment because it's so addictive. Thankfully it's also so easy to make.

You can add dried cranberries or dates to the dry mixture for sweetness and texture.

I've gotten lots of questions about the purchased fried garlic and fried onions; I found them online and now keep them in my pantry all the time. They add so much flavor to dressings and salads and I often throw them into rice. You can also sometimes find them in the spice section of your supermarket. See the photo of the chile oil alongside the Ham and Gruyère Crepes (page 152). ***Makes a small jar***

About 6 ounces (2 cups) stemmed and seeded dried chile pieces (I use árbol, guajillo, and pasilla), processed into flakes (not powder)

2 tablespoons purchased fried garlic

2 tablespoons purchased fried onions

1 tablespoon flaky sea salt, plus more if needed

1 tablespoon brown sugar

1 teaspoon crushed coriander seeds

1 teaspoon umami seasoning (optional)

10 garlic cloves, thinly sliced

2 cups avocado oil

Mix together all the ingredients, except the fresh garlic and oil, in a heatproof bowl.

Combine the fresh garlic and oil in a small, heavy saucepan and bring to a simmer over medium heat. Simmer until the garlic is golden, about 10 minutes, being careful not to burn it. Pour the hot oil, with the garlic, over the chile mixture and allow to cool before serving. Add more salt, if necessary.

Listen. LISTEN. You can absolutely buy pickled jalapeños, but you'll feel oh so good about yourself if you make them from scratch. Also, you can add any vegetable you want here. The more traditional additions are carrots, potato, and cauliflower, but even sweet potatoes, zucchini, or chayote squash would work.

The trick is to make sure you parboil any vegetable you add ONLY for a small amount of time so that it's not mushy. Pickled vegetables need to be crisp. There's nothing worse than a soggy, sweet carrot in your escabèche! See photo alongside Tacos Gobernador (page 77). *Makes about 3 cups*

2 tablespoons flaky sea salt

½ pound fresh jalapeños, seeded, deveined, and sliced lengthwise into strips

1½ cups extra-virgin olive oil

4 garlic cloves, sliced

1 medium white onion, thinly sliced

1 cup distilled white vinegar

15 black peppercorns

4 bay leaves

4 teaspoons crumbled dried oregano

Bring 4 cups of water to a boil in a large pot over high heat. Add 1 tablespoon of salt and the sliced jalapeños and cook for 3 minutes. Remove from the pot with a slotted spoon and drain. Transfer to a glass baking dish.

Heat the olive oil in a large, heavy sauté pan over medium heat. Add the garlic and cook, stirring, until fragrant, about 4 minutes. Add the onion and cook, stirring, until softened but not browned, about 2 minutes. Remove from the heat. Add a drop or two of the vinegar to the oil in the pan; if it spatters, let the oil cool down for a few minutes more and then test it again (repeat until it no longer spatters).

When the oil is cool enough, add the remaining vinegar, peppercorns, bay leaves, oregano, and 1 tablespoon salt. Stir to combine. Return the pan to the heat, bring to a simmer over medium heat, and cook for 3 more minutes. Pour this liquid over the chiles in the baking dish and toss to combine. Let the chiles cool to room temperature. Remove the bay leaves before serving.

JALAPEÑOS *en* ESCABÈCHE

All you need here are chiles and oil to make these crunchy, crisp chiles. The cooking time can vary greatly depending on your choice of chile. I've done this with serrano, jalapeño, and güero chiles. Serranos were absolutely delicious, but I almost died of a coughing attack. Jalapeños, depending on the crop, are at the perfect heat level and are my favorite. If you don't want any heat, you can go with güero chiles. Because of their higher water content (and thicker walls), these take much longer to cook, close to 50 minutes! They are all addictive.

You just have to watch them carefully because they all of a sudden go dark and can very quickly become bitter. I am calling for 2 pounds of chiles as they fry down to a much smaller size, but feel free to halve the recipe.

You can combine serranos and jalapeños (if the jalapeños aren't huge and thick) because they have similar cooking times. Güeros can't be combined with the others.

If you want a different version of the chicharrón, simply add ¾ cup of sliced stemmed shiitake mushrooms, and fry at the same time as the chiles to add a different texture and flavor. This is particularly good with the Poblano and Calabacita Cream Soup (page 167). *Makes about 2 cups*

1 quart vegetable oil

2 pounds fresh serrano and/or jalapeño chiles, or güero chiles, stemmed and cut into ¼-inch rings

2 teaspoons flaky sea salt

Chile-lime powder (optional)

Heat the oil in a large sauté pan over high heat to 350°F. Add your choice of the chiles and lower the heat to medium-low. Cook, stirring frequently, until the chiles turn dark brown, about 35 minutes for smaller chiles and up to 55 for larger chiles.

After 20 minutes of cooking, stir in the salt. When the chiles turn dark (watch them because they turn suddenly!), transfer them to a bowl, using a slotted spoon. Sprinkle with a little chile-lime powder here, if you like! You can strain and reuse the oil once it has cooled down; just remember that it is seasoned.

CHICHARRÓN *de* CHILE

SALSA de MOLCAJETE

Very easy; you just need to know the right order of things because you want to start with the drier and tougher ingredients to grind first, like the garlic and onion. Add the wettest ingredients, like tomatoes, last because they make it much harder to pulverize the denser ingredients like the onion.

Your molcajete needs to be seasoned. I do this by grinding about ¼ cup of uncooked white rice into a powder, three times, in the molcajete. It's a workout but basically you are filling all the little pores in the lava rock. Then, I like to take a halved garlic clove and rub it all over the surface and brush with oil and bake it in a 415°F oven for 1 hour. *Be careful when you take it out.* It's as hot as the sun!

Makes about 1½ cups salsa

2 Roma tomatoes

2 medium tomatillos, husked and rinsed

2 fresh jalapeño chiles

2 garlic cloves, unpeeled

¼ medium white onion, peeled

2 dried chiles de árbol

1 teaspoon flaky sea salt, plus more to taste

In a cast-iron skillet over moderately high heat, dry-roast the tomatoes, tomatillos, jalapeños, garlic, and onion. When the garlic's papery outer skin starts to brown, remove the garlic from the pan and carefully peel it, discarding the skin. Continue to roast the tomatoes, tomatillos, jalapeños, and onion until soft and blackened on all sides. Transfer to a plate to cool, reserving the skillet. Add the dried chiles de árbol to the skillet and toast for about 30 seconds, turning frequently.

Place the garlic in a molcajete and season with the teaspoon of salt. Grind with the pestle until a paste forms. Add the chiles de árbol and grind until they break into tiny pieces. Add the onion and grind. Stem the jalapeños before adding them to the molcajete, and continue to grind. Add the tomatoes and grind until smooth. Add the tomatillos and grind until smooth. Season generously with salt.

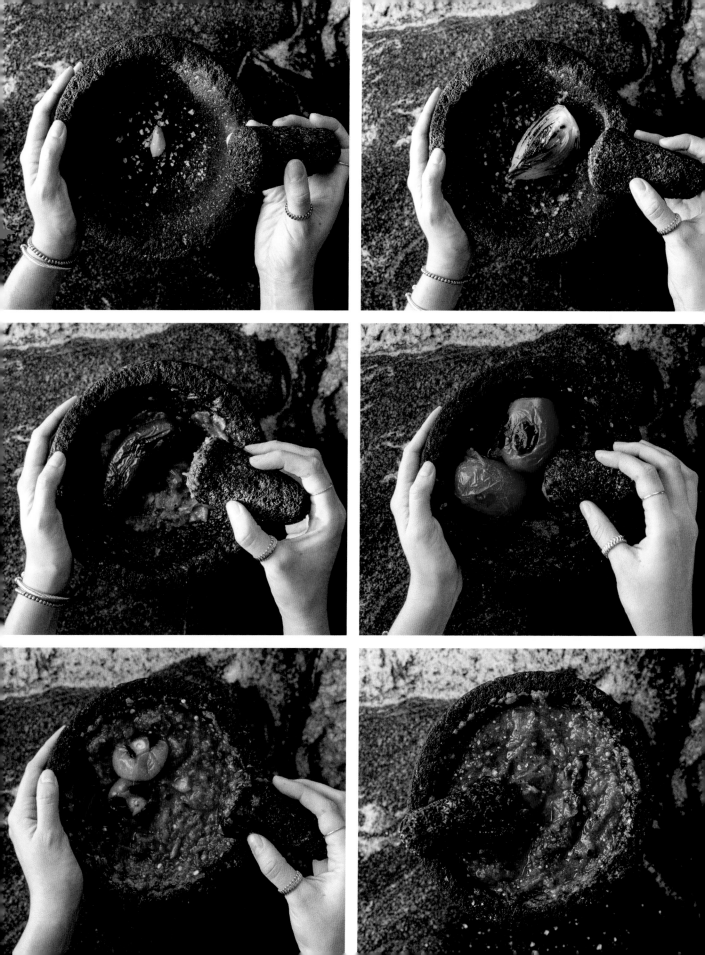

SALSA TAQUERA

This is a very simple salsa with huge flavor. This is the real deal and hot as can be. There are no substitutions or swaps to lower the heat; it's how it is made in Mexico. It has a chile de árbol base, which is pretty hot itself, and then, depending on the cook, may include puya chiles (my preference) or a guajillo or maybe even pumpkin seeds. I've made this with sesame seeds that added a yummy earthy nuttiness. But here you are getting the basics. Some are made with only tomatoes, but I used a combo of tomatoes and tomatillos. See photo with Burritos de Machaca (page 89). ***Makes about 2½ cups***

· · · · · · · · · ·

Listen up because here are some of the most important things you will ever learn about tomatillo-based salsas, and how to prevent them from ending up bitter:

1. Use *fresh* tomatillos. This makes a huge difference. Look for tomatillos whose husks look fresh and not too brown and dry. Stay away from bruised tomatillos or those that have burst open. I didn't understand this until a couple of years ago when I grew them in my garden. The difference in the level of tartness is exponential when they are fresh. You want to move away from a tartness that overpowers what you're eating. The best, least tart flavor comes from the freshest small or medium tomatillos.

2. Rinse the tomatillos well of their sticky residue before you cook them.

3. Adding baking soda to cooking water is thought to balance the pH and remove acidity. If you can only find large tomatillos that you're not sure are the freshest, you will do no harm if you add a pinch of baking soda to your cooking water as a safety measure to avoid that tartness.

4. If you are boiling them, removing them from the water right when they turn olive green is essential. Do not allow them to burst. And don't cook them at a rolling boil. Once the water boils, you can turn off the heat and the tomatillos will continue to cook from the residual heat.

5. The most important tip: wait until the tomatillos are fully cooled down before blending.

· · · · · · · · · ·

10 medium tomatillos, husked and rinsed well

1 medium Roma tomato, cored

2 garlic cloves, peeled

½ cup dried chiles de árbol

2 dried puya chiles

⅓ cup water

¾ teaspoon flaky sea salt

½ medium white onion, chopped (about ½ cup; optional)

⅓ cup chopped fresh cilantro (optional)

Bring 6 cups of water to a boil over high heat. Add the tomatillos, tomato, and garlic and bring back to a boil. Turn off the heat and let the tomatillos sit in the water until they turn olive green. Watch them carefully so they do not burst. Some may be done faster than others. Transfer to a small bowl along with the tomato and garlic cloves. LET COOL COMPLETELY.

Heat a comal or sauté pan over very high heat. Add the chiles de árbol and stir frequently until just toasted and aromatic. Transfer to a blender. Toast the puyas as well, and transfer to the blender. Add the ⅓ cup of water and cooled-down tomatillos, tomato, and garlic. Add the salt. Blend until well combined. Stir in the chopped onion and cilantro, if desired.

A molcajete grinds, releasing oils and aromas, unlike the blade of a food processor or blender when it cuts cut through ingredients. With a molcajete, the result is always more aromatic and flavorful. So, yes, you can use a blender. No, it is not the same. The end.

I'm not trying to be difficult, as much as I enjoy it.

I'm asked all the time where to find an authentic molcajete. Just flip it over and make sure it says "made in Mexico," not China. If it's made in Mexico, it will be lava rock.

The best substitute for a morita chile is a *dried* chipotle (not the stuff in a can). Moritas are slightly less hot than chipotles, with sweeter and more chocolaty notes.

If you plan to make this ahead of time, the most important part is that you don't give up on the disintegration of the skins of both the chiles and the tomatoes. If you get to a point where you want to just eat the darn thing, keep going until you don't have any larger pieces. This takes a while. You will certainly get there much faster with a blender, but the slow method of using the molcajete REALLY brings out the flavor. See photo with Mulitas (page 78). *Makes about 2 cups*

SALSA TAQUERA *de* CHILE MORITA

1 tablespoon extra-virgin olive oil

3 large garlic cloves, peeled

8 dried morita chiles, stemmed and seeded

4 medium tomatillos, husked and well rinsed

2 small Roma tomatoes, cored

1 teaspoon flaky sea salt, plus more if needed

Heat the oil in a small saucepan over medium heat. Add the garlic and moritas and sauté until fragrant, stirring frequently, 1 to 2 minutes. Be careful not to burn the chiles as they will become bitter. Remove from the heat and cool slightly.

Bring a medium saucepan full of salted water to a boil over high heat. Add the tomatillos, tomatoes, plus the toasted garlic and chiles. Bring back to a boil over high heat and boil for 3 minutes. Remove from the heat and let stand for 10 minutes to cool and fully cook the tomatillos until olive green.

Remove the garlic from the water and transfer to a molcajete. Add the salt and mash to a paste. Shaking off any excess liquid, add the soft morita chiles, and mash in the molcajete until fully disintegrated. This takes a while! Banging the tejolote (pestle) onto the molcajete helps! Take all your frustrations out. Then, add the tomatillos, two at a time, mashing slowly to not make them squirt juice. Add the tomatoes and mash. Season the salsa to taste with additional salt, if needed. Serve warm in the molcajete.

This salsa is called bandera because it has the colors of the Mexican flag: green, white, and red. This can be your go-to table salsa because of its ease of preparation and its balanced, iconic flavor. ***Makes 2 cups***

4 Roma tomatoes, seeded and chopped

½ medium white onion, chopped (about ½ cup)

⅓ cup chopped fresh cilantro

1 fresh serrano chile, stemmed, seeded, and chopped

Juice of ½ lime

Flaky sea salt, to taste

Mix together all the ingredients. Serve.

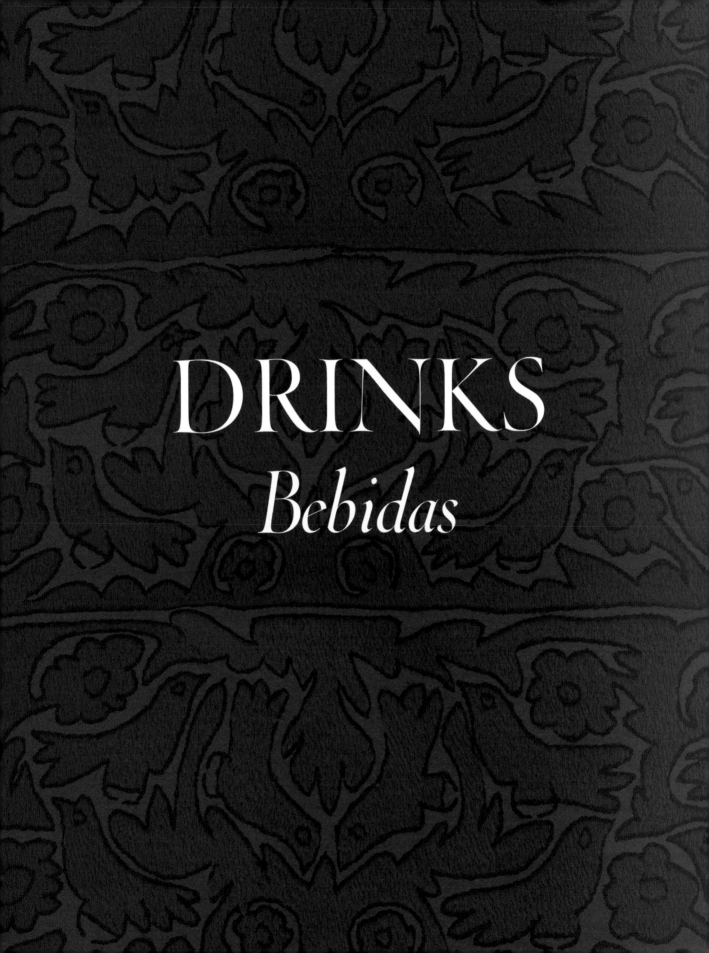

DRINKS
Bebidas

I grew up with jamaica agua fresca in my fridge every day of the year. We didn't drink water, we drank jamaica. It exists in houses all across Mexico and the primary variation is its degree of sweetness. In my house it was *loaded* with sugar. While this definitely does need to be sweetened, you have the option of doing that however you want: sugar, stevia, monk fruit, honey, agave syrup, your choice. Jamaica also has great diuretic properties. ***Makes about 2 quarts***

1 cup granulated sugar

Leaves from 1 bunch mint, plus more for garnish

7 to 9 cups water, divided

Hibiscus concentrate from Tacos de Jamaica (page 34)

Combine the sugar, mint leaves, and 1 cup of the water in a small saucepan over medium heat; stir to dissolve the sugar and infuse the mint flavor, about 5 minutes.

Place the hibiscus concentrate in a pitcher. Strain and add the mint mixture, discarding the leaves. Add the remaining 6 to 8 cups of water to the pitcher, checking to ensure it is not diluting the mixture too much.

Serve over ice. Garnish with mint leaves.

JAMAICA *and* MINT AGUA FRESCA

HORCHATA *de* COCO

Growing up, I wasn't a fan of horchata and its milky texture at all. But I've grown to love it because of its sweet and cinnamon-like flavor that pairs so nicely with Mexican dishes. My method is different from the traditional ways to make horchata (which involve an extra step of straining); I streamlined it by just blending all the ingredients together. But you have to make sure you're working with a high-powered blender that won't leave any large pieces of the cinnamon stick so people don't choke and die! If you don't have a high-powered blender, strain the liquid through a fine-mesh strainer before you serve. *Serves 6 to 8*

2 cups uncooked white rice

2 cinnamon sticks

2 cups water, hot to the touch

2 teaspoons vanilla extract

2 cups canned coconut milk

3 cups sweetened condensed milk, divided

1 cup canned evaporated milk

3 cups water

1 cup shredded coconut, for garnish

In a large bowl, combine the rice, cinnamon sticks, and hot water and let rest for 30 minutes to an hour.

Once the rice has absorbed some of the water, transfer the entire mixture to a high-powered blender and add the vanilla, coconut milk, 2 cups of the condensed milk, and the evaporated milk and blend until fully incorporated. Work in batches if needed. Strain the horchata into a pitcher, discarding any solids, and add the water.

Pour some of the remaining cup of condensed milk into a small plate, and in a second plate, spread the shredded coconut. Rim each serving glass with condensed milk, then with shredded coconut. Serve your horchata in the rimmed glasses.

PRICKLY PEAR *and* LEMONGRASS
AGUA FRESCA *with a Jalapeño Kick*

I used to go running in Beverly Hills when Philip moved there. We'd always run by this giant gorgeous nopal that was smack in the middle of Beverly Hills and I would see so many prickly pears growing on it that would just rot. It was so sad. That's all a prickly pear is, the fruit that grows off the nopal, and it's the best part. Across Mexico, the fruit is known as a tuna, which can be confusing since it has nothing to do with the fish (atún).

Prickly pears can't really be substituted for, but dragon fruit will give you a nice agua fresca and kiwi would also yield a fresh drink! This is a perfect pairing for a smoky Tesmole (page 163). **Serves 4**

To peel a prickly pear:

1. Slice off both ends of the prickly pear. Save them for your compost.

2. Make a slice lengthwise down the body of the prickly pear, about ⅛ inch deep.

3. Wedge your finger in there just under the skin and peel it back.

4 cups water

1 cup granulated sugar (or less; I really like sugar)

1 fresh jalapeño chile, sliced in half

½ cup packed fresh mint leaves

⅔ cup chopped fresh lemongrass stalks, or ⅓ cup dried

6 prickly pears, peeled

Juice of 2 limes

Chile-lime powder (optional)

Combine the water, sugar, jalapeño, mint, and lemongrass in a medium saucepan and simmer for 6 minutes over high heat, or until the flavors blend and the sugar completely dissolves. Remove from the heat and let cool completely. Transfer the mixture to a blender along with the peeled prickly pears and lime juice and blend until smooth. Work in batches as needed. Strain into a pitcher. Rim the top of your glasses with chile-lime powder before serving, if you like. Serve the agua fresca over ice.

WATERMELON, JALAPEÑO, and MINT AGUA FRESCA

As an adult, I've embraced spice in an agua fresca. It makes it somehow crisper and almost more fresh. Trust me, the jalapeño works here. I'm with you if you don't like tradition messed with and you just want an agua fresca like the kind you got when you ditched school and went to the frutería behind your other friend's school in Tijuana. (Okay, that was a bit personal, but you get my drift.) Try it. You'll love it. Plus, the thyme and mint really balance it out. *Serves 6 to 8*

½ cup granulated sugar

¾ cup loosely packed fresh mint leaves

½ cup water

½ fresh jalapeño chile, stemmed and seeded

2 thyme sprigs

5 cups chopped, seeded watermelon

Combine the sugar, mint, and water in a medium saucepan and cook over medium heat until the sugar dissolves, about 4 minutes. Add the jalapeño and thyme and let infuse for 5 minutes.

Remove the jalapeño and mint, and set the sugary thyme sprigs aside to use as a garnish. Strain the infusion and transfer, along with the watermelon, to a blender. Blend until very smooth, about 2 minutes. Serve cold over ice and garnish with the sugary sprigs of thyme.

PINEAPPLE-BASIL AGUA FRESCA
(or, perhaps, Calientito de Piña y Albahaca)

What on earth is she talking about in this recipe title, you say? Well, maybe not everyone lives in California with average temperatures of 70°F year-round. I wanted to create a drink that would give the option to those folks, say in Chicago, to heat this baby up, add some diced fruit (and whatever else makes you happy), and serve as a calientito (hot drink). I used fresh pineapple but frozen pineapple works too. The amount of sugar (i.e., syrup) you add totally depends on the natural, existing sugar in your pineapple of choice. See the variation following the directions for how to serve hot. *Serves 4 to 6*

1 cup granulated sugar

2 cups water, divided

5 to 8 large basil leaves

1 pineapple, peeled, cored, and cut into ½-inch pieces (about 4 cups)

1 cinnamon stick, torn into small pieces

1 teaspoon vanilla extract

½ cup coconut milk (*not* coconut water)

Combine the sugar and 1 cup of the water in a small saucepan. Bring to a boil over high heat, swirling the pan to dissolve the sugar. Add the basil and cook for 3 minutes. Turn off the heat and let stand until cool. Remove the basil leaves. Set the basil syrup aside.

Place the chopped pineapple in a blender along with the remaining cup of water, cinnamon stick pieces, vanilla, and coconut milk. Blend on high speed for about 4 minutes, or until very smooth. Add ¼ to ½ cup of the basil syrup. Save the remaining syrup for another use, or add all of it if you're like Elf and have maple syrup for breakfast. Using a fine-mesh strainer, strain the agua fresca into a pitcher or large bowl. Serve over plenty of ice.

HOW TO SERVE HOT

I love serving things in edible vessels so why not use Anjou pears? My suggestion is to purchase 6 to 8 *firm* Anjou pears, cut off the stem and about ½ inch from the top. Using a melon baller or a small spoon, carefully scoop out the center of each pear to create cups, being careful not to pierce the bottom of the pears. Chop the scooped pear into equal-size pieces and chop an additional pear into cubes. Bring the prepared agua fresca to a boil in a medium saucepan over high heat, then turn off the heat. Very carefully, pour the hot drink into pears and garnish each with a few pieces of chopped pear.

For the mangoes, look for the ripest around—and honestly, skip this recipe if you can't find any. There's almost nothing worse than a pale yellow and tart mango. They need to be almost orangey yellow and soft to the touch. *Serves 6*

6 cups water, divided

1½ cups granulated sugar, or to taste, divided

1 cup fresh mint leaves, plus more for garnish

4 ripe mangoes

Combine 1 cup of the water with 1 cup of the sugar and the mint in a medium saucepan and bring to a boil over high heat. Mix well to dissolve the sugar. Strain, set aside, and let the mint syrup cool.

Peel the mangoes. Slice as much of the mango away from the pits as you can. Throw away the pits. Place the sliced mango in a blender with ½ cup of the sugar (or more, depending on the ripeness of the mangoes) and 3 cups of the water and blend until smooth. Strain the mango water into a pitcher and add mint syrup to taste. Add 1 to 2 cups of the remaining water to dilute to your desired consistency. Serve over ice. Garnish with mint.

MANGO-MINT AGUA FRESCA

When you smell this, there's never any confusion about what's on the stove. Café de la olla has such a unique and recognizable aroma that it's like a warm hug that takes me immediately back home to Mexico when I smell it. *Serves 4 to 6*

· · · · · · · · · ·

There are a few key elements to a successful café de la olla:

1. Don't cook this at a rolling boil, to prevent the ingredients from becoming bitter.

2. You *absolutely* must use a fine-mesh strainer and line it with cheesecloth or a drip coffee filter (or even a paper towel). You cannot let a single grain of coffee into your coffee cup when you serve. It is not allowed.

3. Make sure it's piping hot, and preferably serve it with a concha for dunking. See photo alongside the Huevos Divorciados (page 133).

· · · · · · · · · ·

⅔ cup ground dark-roasted coffee, medium to coarse grind

1 quart water

1 8-ounce piloncillo cone

1 cinnamon stick, plus more for garnish (optional)

1 3-inch piece orange peel

4 whole cloves (optional)

Halved orange slices, for garnish (optional)

In a medium saucepan over medium heat, combine the ground coffee with the water, piloncillo, cinnamon stick, orange peel, and cloves (if using). Bring to a simmer, stirring to dissolve the sugar. Remove from the heat and let steep, covered, for 5 minutes. Strain through a lined fine-mesh strainer into cups and serve. If desired, you can garnish each cup with a halved orange slice and a cinnamon stick.

There's no singular list of ingredients that make a ponche navideño; by definition it's just a hot fruit drink—you decide the fruit. The more traditional ingredients are piloncillo, guavas, and cinnamon, but you can pretty much add anything you want after that. Just about any fresh or dried fruit can go into the mix and it'll work. I don't mention pears in the recipe, but they're great, as are lemon peels and pineapple, and dried mangoes, apples, and prunes. I don't like to add anything that might make the drink too acidic, but if that's your preference, that's fine too.

Tejocotes (hawthorn fruit) are sold both fresh and jarred in syrup. If you have access to a Mexican market, tejocotes will be usually available at the winter season because ponche navideño is such a mandatory beverage during the holidays. They look like a small guava but have the taste of a crab apple.

This recipe makes a lot; you could cut it in half for a smaller party. *Makes 2 gallons*

2 gallons water

3 tamarind pods, peeled

2 apples, cut into eighths and cored

4 cinnamon sticks

1 8-ounce piloncillo cone

2 cups dried hibiscus flowers

6 guavas, top core removed, quartered

10 or 12 tejocotes, top core removed, halved

A few pieces of sugarcane (optional)

In a large pot, bring the water to a boil over high heat. Add the tamarind pods, apples, cinnamon sticks, piloncillo, and hibiscus. Boil for 10 minutes. Add the guava and tejocotes and continue to cook until softened and fragrant. The aroma is to die for. For real. Add the sugarcane. I always do.

Ladle some ponche and fruit into a cup and serve.

PONCHE NAVIDEÑO

PONCHE NAVIDEÑO

DESSERTS
Postres

Fluffy PINEAPPLE TAMALES

These are considered a breakfast pastry or a dessert and found across Mexico. Any place with a decent tamal menu will have a sweet option, and 90 percent of the time, that sweet option will be pineapple. If you did it right, they're light and pillowy, and before you know it, you've eaten twelve.

You must be patient and whip, whip, whip the masa so you add enough air to make those tamales fluffy. You need a lot of experience (and time) to do this by hand, so we use a hand mixer instead. You can use a stand mixer if it has a large enough bowl.

You can use fresh pineapple, but canned allows me to give you a more precise recipe. The sweetness, texture, and moisture of a pineapple can vary greatly, which can compromise your recipe. I suggest you stick with canned to get a feel of what the masa should look and feel like, and then start experimenting. Even a perfect recipe won't give you what experience gives you when making tamales.

Vegetable shortening and butter are our fat base. Lard is an option if you don't want to keep it plant-based. For this recipe, we're using Maseca instead of an heirloom or artisan ground masa harina, because it's easy to purchase and will give you consistent results. Try it first with Maseca, and then experiment.

You know the tamal is done when you can peel back the husk from the masa without its sticking or crumbling. That's why you must place the masa on the smooth side of the husk during assembly.

Note: You can use any steamer pot, but a tamal steamer is best because you can stack so many tamales in at one time. ***Makes 30 tamales***

---

1 pound vegetable shortening (I use Crisco), at room temperature

½ pound (2 sticks) unsalted butter, at room temperature

4 cups Maseca (masa harina)

2 20-ounce cans pineapple chunks (drained and minced, about 3 cups), ½ cup juice reserved

1¾ to 2 cups granulated sugar

1 teaspoon baking powder

Pinch of flaky sea salt

30 to 35 corn husks, individually washed, soaked in hot water 30 minutes

---

Have ready a large steamer filled with water to just below the rack.

Place the shortening in a large bowl, then, using an electric mixer, whip until lightened in color and very fluffy, about 5 minutes. Add the butter and whip for 5 minutes longer. Gradually add the masa harina until well incorporated.

In a small saucepan, heat the reserved pineapple juice with the sugar, stirring just to dissolve. Once dissolved, gradually add the juice mixture to the masa a little at a time, continuing to beat for 5 minutes. Add the baking powder and a pinch of salt and beat for 1 minute longer. Add the 3 cups of minced pineapple chunks and beat for 4 minutes.

Take a heaping soup spoon of masa and place in the center of a corn husk, more toward one of the edges. Corn husks have smooth and rough sides; place the masa on the smoother side. Enclose the masa and fold the pointy bottom up. You can use a string of husk to tie the tamal for a nice presentation. Repeat until you have formed 30 tamales.

Place in the prepared steamer, overlapping the tamales in circles. Once all the tamales are in the steamer, cover with additional corn husks and then a clean kitchen towel to ensure steam does not escape. Cover with the steamer lid and steam the tamales for 1 hour. Turn off the heat and let cool in the steamer for 30 minutes. The masa should easily separate from its corn husk when the tamale is opened. Try not to eat them all in one sitting, but you might. That's just what happens.

This recipe was developed by my trusted and regular photographer Isabella while I was busy birthing and nursing babies, and she steered the ship while developing recipes for the blog! Pretty sure this was developed for a TV show, too, but that whole time is kind of a blur, to be honest. I sometimes look back and have no idea how some things got done considering I was either pregnant or nursing for over three years straight.

But enough about me, let's talk about mangoes. Make sure they are RIPE. Still firm enough where they'll hold their shape, but ripe and sweet, and for the love of this cake, not that pale yellow color of the packaged presliced mango they sell you at the supermarket.

There are usually just two kinds at the US markets. Tommy Atkins are red, green, and orange on the outside and bigger. When ripe, these are great but are a little more fibrous than the second variety, Ataulfo mangoes. Those are generally a solid yellow/orange color and on the smaller side. I prefer their flavor and silkier texture but they might not yield the prettiest slices for the upside-down cake! Totally up to you.

The only potentially daunting thing here is making the caramel sauce. Fear not: if you mess it up, we will blame it on your children interrupting you during the process, never on my instruction. Godspeed. *Serves 6*

Unsalted butter, for the pan

½ cup packed light brown sugar

12 tablespoons (1½ sticks) unsalted butter, at room temperature

2 large mangoes, peeled, pitted, and cut into ½-inch slices (about 2 cups)

½ cup sweetened shredded coconut

2¼ cups all-purpose flour

4 teaspoons baking powder

1 teaspoon flaky sea salt

1½ cups granulated sugar

3 large eggs

1 teaspoon vanilla extract

1¼ cups whole milk

Place a rack in the middle of oven; preheat to 350°F. Butter a 9-inch springform pan; set aside.

In a small saucepan, combine the brown sugar and 4 tablespoons of the butter over medium heat. Stir constantly until the sugar dissolves and the syrup bubbles; boil until it turns light amber. Immediately remove from the heat and carefully pour into the prepared springform pan. Arrange the mango slices on top and sprinkle with the coconut; set aside.

In a medium bowl, whisk together the flour, baking powder, and salt; then set aside.

In a large bowl, beat the remaining 8 tablespoons of butter and the granulated sugar with an electric mixer on high speed for 6 minutes, or until light and fluffy. Add the eggs, one at a time, beating well after each addition. Beat in the vanilla. Add half of the flour mixture; beat on low speed until just combined. Beat in the milk, then the remaining flour mixture until combined.

Gently spoon the batter over the mango slices; spread evenly. Place the springform pan on a baking sheet. Bake for 1 hour, or until golden brown and a tester inserted into the center comes out clean.

Remove from the oven and let cool on a wire rack for 10 minutes. Run a knife around the inside edge of the pan. Set a plate over the cake and then invert the cake onto the plate. Let cool completely on the plate; serve at room temperature.

MANGO UPSIDE-DOWN CAKE

FRESAS con CREMA

This quintessential Mexican dessert is so simple, so straightforward, and loved by adults and kids alike. This is a vegan version; the traditional one uses sweetened condensed milk. I promise you won't miss the dairy, and you will love making this for your kids. Any other berry will work with this!

As ever when blending cashews, you *must* soak them in water for at least overnight before you blend them. I soak for two days to really soften them, and use a high-powered blender. **Makes about 3 cups crema for 6 servings**

1½ cups raw unsalted cashews, soaked in water overnight and drained

1 cup coconut milk

¼ cup water

Fine zest of 1 lemon

1 teaspoon freshly squeezed lemon juice

2 teaspoons vanilla extract

2 tablespoons pure maple syrup

5 to 6 cups strawberries, stemmed and quartered (or other berries)

Granola or pepitas, for serving (optional)

Date syrup, for serving (optional)

Place the drained cashews, coconut milk, water, lemon zest and juice, vanilla, and maple syrup in a blender and blend until very, very smooth; this is your crema. Divide the strawberries among six serving cups, then pour the crema over the berries. Here you can have a little fun; crunchy granola or pepitas are a great garnish. I like things sweet, so I drizzle with date syrup.

Cajeta is similar to caramel, but it's not so cloyingly sweet because it's made with goat's milk. It has a savory tinge that, dangerously, means you can eat a lot more of it. You will find endless varieties of it; Cajeta Coronado is a readily available brand. You can use dulce de leche as a substitute, but you should definitely try cajeta if you never have before.

Ideally you have a 7½-inch nonstick crepe pan, but honestly, any good nonstick pan will work. The only thing that will vary is the size of your crepes and, therefore, the yield. I used a 9-inch pan and got six VERY large crepes and that also works.

To toast pecans: Preheat the oven to 350°F and line a large rimmed baking sheet with parchment paper or a silicone mat. Arrange the pecans in a single layer and roast for 5 to 10 minutes, stirring or shaking the pan occasionally so the nuts brown evenly without burning. Note: Do not walk away and leave your pecans unattended.

Makes 6 to 8 crepas

1 cup all-purpose flour

2 tablespoons granulated sugar

½ cup whole milk

2 tablespoons unsalted butter, melted and cooled

3 large eggs

1 teaspoon orange zest (optional)

Pinch of flaky sea salt

Cooking spray or unsalted butter, for the pan

FOR SERVING

½ to ¾ cup cajeta, warmed with 2 tablespoons milk (to make pourable)

1 cup pecans, toasted and chopped

Combine the flour, sugar, milk, butter, and eggs in a blender. Blend for 10 seconds, then scrape down the sides and blend until smooth, about 20 seconds longer. Transfer to a bowl and stir in the orange zest, if using, and salt. Let stand at room temperature for 30 minutes.

Heat a crepe pan over medium heat. Spray with cooking spray or brush with butter. If the batter is thick, add 1 to 2 tablespoons of water; it should be pretty runny! Add a scant ladleful of batter to the pan and swirl the pan to evenly cover the bottom of the pan with the batter. Cook until just set, then flip the crepe. Ideally, there are no brown spots on the crepe, but it's okay if there are. Wipe the pan with paper towels between crepes, spraying or buttering again as necessary.

Fold each crepe in half, then in half again to form a rounded triangle. Place the crepes on individual plates and top with cajeta and toasted pecans. Strawberries can be added too!

CREPAS *with* CAJETA

Elsa's BROWNIES

There's not much to say except these are just the best basic brownies ever. There's nothing particularly Mexican about them. They're just great brownies.

The recipe comes from one of my sister Carina's childhood best friends, renowned Baja pastry chef Elsa Flores. Her pastry shop Dolce Salato (@dolcesalatotj on Instagram) has some of the most delicious cakes in all of Baja. The carrot cake is insane. The coconut roulade is heaven on a plate. The red velvet it to die for, and everything she makes with chocolate is addictive. We get some of her home-style cooking with these easy brownies, but she is classically trained and ridiculously talented. We love you, Elsa! *Makes a 9-inch square pan of brownies*

Cooking spray, for the foil

6 ounces semisweet chocolate, chopped

8 tablespoons (1 stick) unsalted butter

1 cup granulated sugar

3 large eggs

1 cup all-purpose flour

½ teaspoon baking powder

¼ teaspoon flaky sea salt

2 ounces bittersweet chocolate, cut into pieces

Position an oven rack in the middle of the oven and preheat to 350°F. Line a 9-inch square baking pan with foil and spray with cooking spray.

Melt the semisweet chocolate and butter in a medium heatproof bowl set atop a saucepan partially filled with water (it should not touch the bottom of the bowl). Simmer over medium-low heat, stirring occasionally, until smooth.

In a stand mixer fitted with the whisk attachment, beat together the sugar and eggs on medium-high speed until fluffy, about 3 minutes. Pour in the chocolate mixture and whisk until well combined. Mix in the flour, baking powder, and salt for about 2 minutes on medium speed. Stir in the bittersweet chocolate chunks and transfer the batter to the prepared baking pan.

Bake until the top is shiny and set, and the sides have begun to pull away slightly, about 35 minutes for fudgy brownies. Remove from the oven and let cool in the pan before slicing.

I grew up eating chamoy as candy. It's a pourable smooth sauce made from cooked-down fruit, usually stone fruit, and sugar, spiced with chiles, lime or citric acid, and salt. I would squirt it on potato chips as a snack. It's a great dip to get kids to eat fruit if they're into that flavor profile. It's also great for moistening the rims of glassware before applying salt or spice. Chamoy is something I am totally cool with you purchasing, not making from scratch. One day, you will make chamoy. Today will not be the day.

If you don't have an ice pop mold, use small paper cups and put ice pop sticks in them, secured on the outside with tape. *Makes 6 to 8 paletas*

1 cup water

1 cup granulated sugar

4 cups chopped ripe mango (from 8 or 9 pitted and peeled mangoes)

¼ cup chamoy sauce

¼ cup chile-lime powder

Bring the water to a boil over high heat. Add the sugar and stir to dissolve. Let cool completely.

Place 3 cups of the chopped mango in a blender along with the sugar water and puree until smooth. Reserve the remaining mango chunks to add to the mold.

Add a couple of tablespoons each of chamoy and chile-lime powder, and 2 or 3 of the mango chunks, to your mold, then add your mango puree, and repeat with the remaining chamoy and chile-lime powder, until your mold is full.

Cover and freeze for about 4 hours, preferably overnight. I like to squeeze a little lime juice over the top and sprinkle with extra chile-lime powder when eating!

MANGO-CHAMOY PALETAS

This is a showstopper that's actually very easy to make as long as you follow the instructions. Cleaning the mixer with vinegar is a *must* every single time you make this. Fine sugar is much more forgiving to the inexperienced meringue-maker, so use that. Invest in a silicone mat. I use mine a lot; Silpats are my favorite.

Instead of making one large Pavlova, you can make individual servings by drawing eight 3½ -inch-diameter circles on parchment paper, then flip the paper and place on the baking sheet. Follow the instructions below, but divide the meringue into 8 mounds on the circles. *Serves 8 to 10*

4 large egg whites, at room temperature (reserve yolks for another use)

½ teaspoon cream of tartar

Pinch of flaky sea salt

2 teaspoons vanilla extract

1 cup granulated sugar, processed until superfine

1½ teaspoons cornstarch

1¾ cups whipping cream, cold

¼ cup powdered sugar

¼ cup cajeta

1 tablespoon vanilla extract

1 pint strawberries

1 cup raspberries

1 cup blackberries

Leaves from 1 mint sprig (optional)

TIP: When separating your eggs, work with one at a time. That way, if you accidentally pierce a yolk, you don't have to discard all the whites and start again. It's important to not get any yolk into the whites!

Preheat the oven to 300°F. Use a plate, bowl, or cake pan to draw a circle between 7 and 8 inches in diameter on a sheet of parchment paper. Place the paper, drawn side down, on a large rimmed baking sheet and set aside. If using a silicone mat, you can dip the edges of an 8-inch-diameter plate in flour and then flip the plate on the mat to make a flour circle and use that as your guide.

Combine the egg whites, cream of tartar, salt, and vanilla in the bowl of a *clean* stand mixer (use a cloth with distilled white vinegar to fully clean it) fitted with the whisk attachment and mix on medium-low speed.

Once the egg whites are frothy, you can begin sprinkling in the sugar, a few tablespoons at a time. The key is not to dump the sugar in, but to add it very slowly. You are looking for a very glossy and marshmallowy texture.

Sprinkle the cornstarch onto the meringue and fold in, using a rubber spatula.

Transfer your meringue to the center of the prepared baking sheet and use a spatula to spread it evenly to fill your circle, with a ½-inch-deep dent in the center.

Place in the oven and immediately lower the temperature to 275°F. Bake for 1 hour. It should be firm on the outside. If not, leave in for 15 minutes longer. Turn off the heat and allow the meringue to sit in the oven while it cools for at least 1 hour or overnight.

Combine the cream, powdered sugar, cajeta, and vanilla in the bowl of your cleaned stand mixer fitted with a whisk attachment (or use an electric hand mixer). Mix on high speed until soft peaks form. Transfer the cream to the center of the meringue. Garnish with the berries. You can add mint leaves and/or sift powdered sugar over the top, if desired.

CAJETA BROWNIES

These brownies come from the creator of the first cake bar (where you build own cake) in Mexico, pastry chef Dani Flores. You can use semisweet chocolate chips, but it will not have that rich dense chocolate taste. I mean, chocolate is chocolate; they will be great, but not the elevated brownie we are looking for. The cajeta adds another layer of sweetness and enough pizzazz to be the dessert for an evening of entertaining, with a scoop of ice cream. *Makes nine 2½-inch brownie squares*

5 ounces dark chocolate (any chocolate from 55 to 74%), chopped, divided

8 tablespoons (1 stick) unsalted butter, cut into small chunks

¼ cup unsweetened cocoa powder

½ teaspoon baking powder

¼ cup all-purpose flour

1¼ teaspoons flaky sea salt, divided

2 large eggs

¾ cup granulated sugar

1 cup cajeta

Preheat the oven to 350°F. Line the bottom and sides of an 8-inch square cake pan with parchment paper.

Melt 3 ounces of the dark chocolate and the butter together in a medium heatproof bowl set over a saucepan, making sure the water doesn't touch the bottom of the bowl. When they are melted, remove the bowl from the heat and stir well to combine. Let cool for about 5 minutes.

In a small bowl, combine the cocoa powder, baking powder, flour, and ¼ teaspoon of the salt; set aside.

In a separate medium bowl, whisk together the eggs and sugar until light and creamy, about 2 minutes.

Whisking constantly, add the chocolate mixture to the egg mixture and whisk until well combined. Add the flour mixture and gently fold with a spatula just until combined, then add the remaining 2 ounces of chopped dark chocolate.

Pour half of the brownie batter into the prepared pan. Use a tablespoon to add dollops of half of the cajeta all over the surface of the brownie batter. Run a small sharp knife or skewer through the batter to create a marbled effect. Repeat by adding the remaining brownie batter, dolloping with the remaining cajeta, and again creating the marbled effect.

Sprinkle the remaining teaspoon of salt on top and bake until the brownies are dry on top but still slightly gooey and fudgy inside, 30 minutes.

Remove from the oven, let cool, unmold, and cut into squares.

Making buñuelos from scratch is not that easy. It's like learning how to make flour tortillas—you need a few tries to become comfortable rolling them out to paper thin without tearing them. The only thing that gets you there is experience. So, don't be upset if they don't come out perfect on the first try, in terms of presentation. Even if they are thick, broken, or not that presentable, they're still going to taste good.

You have the option of bypassing this whole process and purchasing precooked flour tortillas, which can double as masa. They are labeled as "precocidas" at your Mexican market. *Makes about 16 buñuelos*

10 fresh culinary lavender flowers

1 8-ounce piloncillo cone

1 cup water

Peel of 1 orange

1²/₃ cups all-purpose flour, plus ¼ cup for dusting

½ cup plus 1 tablespoon granulated sugar, divided

1 tablespoon baking powder

½ teaspoon flaky sea salt

1 large egg

1 tablespoon unsalted butter, at room temperature

1 teaspoon vanilla extract

⅓ to ½ cup warm water

Vegetable oil, for resting dough and frying

1 teaspoon ground cinnamon

Combine the lavender, piloncillo, water, and orange peel in a small, heavy saucepan and bring to a boil over high heat to dissolve the piloncillo. Lower the heat to low and let cook for 30 minutes to infuse the flavors. Remove from the heat, let cool slightly, then strain, discarding any solids.

Place the 1²/₃ cups of flour in a large bowl. Whisk in 1 tablespoon of the sugar, plus the baking powder and salt. Make a well in the center and add the egg, butter, and vanilla. Using your fingertips, mix until coarse crumbs form. Add the warm water, a couple of tablespoons at a time, until the dough comes together but is not too sticky. Turn out the dough onto a lightly floured surface and knead until smooth and shiny, about 5 minutes.

Place a little oil on your fingertips and coat all of the surface of the dough with a little oil. Place in a medium bowl, cover tightly with plastic wrap, and let stand at room temperature (not too cold) for 30 minutes.

Divide into 15 or 16 balls, about a tablespoon of dough each. I use a scale, and each is about 1 ounce, but you can eyeball them. Coat each ball lightly with oil again and cover with plastic wrap. Let stand for 10 minutes.

Pour enough vegetable oil into a large skillet to come ¹/₂ inch up the sides of the pan, and heat to 350°F. Working one at a time, on a floured surface, roll each dough ball into a paper-thin disk, using a rolling pin and constantly rotating. Fry each individually until golden brown, turning occasionally. Transfer to paper towels to drain.

Mix together the remaining ¹/₂ cup of sugar and the cinnamon in a small bowl and transfer to a small baking sheet. Lightly sprinkle each side of the buñuelos with the sugar mixture. One by one, stand a buñuelo upright in the sugar mixture and carefully pour additional sugar all over it. Serve with the syrup.

BUÑUELOS *with Lavender Syrup*

BUÑUELOS WITH LAVENDER SYRUP

MENU OPTIONS

Although I have presented these recipes in sections for you to pick and choose from as you like, I originally developed them for cooking classes. I paired specific recipes together to form interesting menus that could be cooked in a reasonable amount of time.

If you get the mise en place (prep work) done, each of these menus can be executed within two hours. We did that live every single class: it really can be done! But it's like making Thanksgiving dinner: you must program yourself to cook three dishes at once. That skill is as important to me to teach as any single recipe. That skill is what I really want students to learn.

So, how do you do it? If you read a recipe that needs two hours to make, start with that one instead of with the salad. Don't think about executing what's easiest first. Instead, organize your time according to what each recipe needs.

EAT, PRAY, LOVE

*Creamy Chipotle Spaghetti with
Cilantro-Parmesan Croutons (page 113)*

Sopa de Albóndigas (page 172)

Mango Upside-Down Cake (page 239)

COWBOY/COWGIRL
VALENTINE'S DAY

*Pollo con Papas with Arugula Salsa Verde
(page 151)*

Entomatadas (page 96)

Cajeta Brownies (page 252)

CHEF MARCELA'S
MARIACHI BIRTHDAY
PARTY

*Ham and Gruyère Crepes
with Poblano Sauce (page 152)*

Mango-Mint Agua Fresca (page 229)

Mango-Chamoy Paletas (page 247)

Cajeta Pavlovas (page 248)

FATHER'S DAY

El Perfect Ribeye (page 137)

*Superdecadent Creamy Potato Cake
(page 194)*

*Brussels Sprouts with Guajillos and
Piloncillo-Caramelized Pancetta (page 190)*

Elsa's Brownies (page 244)

HEALTHY MEXICAN,
'90S SPANDEX EDITION

*Plant-Based Potato Latkes and Salsa Verde
(page 115)*

*Plant-Based Enchiladas with "Creamy"
Chipotle Salsa (page 119)*

*Iceberg Salad Garnish for Any Mexican Dish
(page 120)*

Fresas con Crema (page 240)

BAJA STYLE

Tacos de Salmón (page 129)

Salsa Bandera (page 217)

Cabbage Slaw (page 130)

Tacos de Jamaica (page 34)

Jamaica and Mint Agua Fresca (page 221)

DÍA DE LA CANDELARIA

Bacalao a la Vizcaina (page 81)

Wedge Salad with Blue Cheese and Chipotle Caramelized Pecans (page 42)

Corn-Studded Fluffy White Rice (page 182)

MOLE

Mole Poblano (see Shredded Mole Chicken Tacos recipe, page 84)

Arroz Rojo (page 186)

Cucumber-Mint Salad (page 51)

Corn Tortillas (page 198)

CHILES EN NOGADA (VALLE)

Chiles en Nogada (page 66) and Cashew Nogada Sauce (page 67)

Hatch Chiles Stuffed with Calabacitas (page 110)

Roasted Beet Salad with Macha Pecans (page 41)

FALL EDITION

Tesmole (page 163)

Poblano and Calabacita Cream Soup (page 167)

Prickly Pear and Lemongrass Agua Fresca with a Jalapeño Kick (page 225)

CHRISTMAS POSADA

Chipotle Chilaquiles (page 71)

Fluffy Pineapple Tamales (page 236)

TACOS DE JAMAICA

ACKNOWLEDGMENTS

Muchas gracias…

To my sister Carina, for doing that thing that you've done my whole life: making me feel loved and talented and worthy and ready. I never would have done these classes if I hadn't known you'd be there with me. Not because I didn't think I could, but because I knew that doing it next to you it wouldn't feel like work. That it would be an absolute blast. I was right. But that's the energy you bring to everything. Gracias. Te adoro.

To the folks that made publishing this collection of recipes possible: Rica Allanic, my lit agent. Fifteen years later, here we are. Together again. Mike Szczerban, this was unequivocally the easiest book I've ever done and that was because of your guidance. Thank you, Voracious, for this opportunity.

My team at home that helped bring these recipes to the thousands of students. Vane Garza and Anna Sofia Otañez, every single time you guys walked in here with the intention of putting out *the very best* show, every time it felt like we did. Jorge Pérez Flores and your production crew Sergio Fernandez, Alejandra Villanueva, and Ángel Gabriel Morales.

To the ladies that helped put this book together. I have so much love and admiration for all of you. Isabella Martinez-Funcke, my favorite photog on earth. Erika Funcke, for your styling perfection. Valerie Aikman-Smith, for your accurate and beautiful execution of all the recipes. All of the assistants, Debora Contreras, Natalia Ruvalcaba, Veronica Laramie, and Ariella Azair. Elvia Felix, for always making me look my best. Claudia Nicole Herrera, for the perfect pony.

Huge thanks to Hans Kritzler of Anfora Mexico and his faithful manager of operations, Carlos Vicente, who generously sent us twenty boxes of their gorgeous handcrafted pieces all the way from Mexico City so we could plate this food!

Mi familia hermosa. Felipe, el amor de mi vida AND my manager. Mis hijos, Fausto Antonio, David, Anna Carina, Kongo, and Marcelo el gato. Son mi motor.

My mom, for continuing to be my biggest inspiration and guide, even from another realm.

An enormous thank-you to the familia and every single student that took those classes. It has been my absolute joy to teach and connect with you these past couple of years.

But here's the deal: It took a lot of self-work to reach the courage it took to cook with no fear, so to quote the best "thank-you" speech ever given (by Snoop): "I wanna thank me for believing in me. I wanna thank me for doing all this hard work."

Hasta la próxima, familia…

INDEX

Note: Page references in *italics* indicate photographs.

ABOUT THE AUTHOR

MARCELA VALLADOLID is an Emmy-nominated celebrity chef, television personality, designer, author, mother, and businesswoman. She is the founder and CEO of the artisanal Mexican housewares brand Casa Marcela, Inc., and the author of five previous cookbooks. Having grown up around expert and traditional cooks in Tijuana, Mexico, Marcela began her career as a food editor for *Bon Appétit*. She co-hosted the hit Food Network show *The Kitchen* and *The Marcela & Carina Show*, a virtual live cooking show with her sister, Carina Valladolid. She has been featured in the *Wall Street Journal*, the *New York Times*, *People*, *Food & Wine*, and on television shows including *Today*, *The Talk*, *The Chew*, and *The View*. She resides in Chula Vista, California, with her partner, Philip Button, their three children (Fausto, David, and Anna Carina), and their cat, Marcelo, and dog, Kongo.

Voracious / Little, Brown and Company
Hachette Book Group
1290 Avenue of the Americas
New York, NY 10104
voraciousbooks.com

First Edition: October 2023

Voracious is an imprint of Little, Brown and Company, a division of Hachette Book Group, Inc. The Voracious name and logo are trademarks of Hachette Book Group, Inc.

The publisher is not responsible for websites (or their content) that are not owned by the publisher.

The Hachette Speakers Bureau provides a wide range of authors for speaking events. To find out more, go to hachettespeakersbureau.com or email HachetteSpeakers@hbgusa.com.

Little, Brown and Company books may be purchased in bulk for business, educational, or promotional use. For information, please contact your local bookseller or the Hachette Book Group Special Markets Department at special.markets@hbgusa.com.

Photography by Isabella Martinez-Funcke
Book design by Mia Johnson

Cover and chapter opener textile by Pensamientos o Claveles, represented by Carmina Marruffo Tenorio, from San Bartolomé Ayautla in the Mazateca region in the state of Oaxaca, representing the iconography of the Tree of Life; p. 18: kitchen island by AD HOC Mexico; p. 21: tortilla press by T and H Tortilla Press; p. 38: huipil by Mexicanartes; p. 56: spoon rest by Perro y Arena; p. 69: barro plates by Taller Ruíz López; p. 88: huipil top by Remigio Mestas; p. 144: ceramic bowl by Valerie Aikman-Smith; p. 251: textile chair by Folk Project

ISBN 9780316437905
LCCN 2023935737

10 9 8 7 6 5 4 3 2 1

WOR

Printed in the United States of America